CONTENTS

Introduction

Ch.1 The Early Days **15**
Negative feelings towards the child 16
Coping with emotions 17
Reactions of others in your life 18
Reactions of siblings 19
Useful contacts 21

Ch.2 The Law and Disability **23**
The law and disability 23
The Equality Act 2010 24
Definition of 'impairment' 25
Persons with HIV infection, cancer and multiple sclerosis 26
Definition of 'long-term effects' 28
Normal day-to-day activities 29
Specialised activities 32
Disabled children 34
Useful contacts 36

Ch.3 Professionals and Organisations That You and Your Child Might be Involved With **39**
Clinical psychologist 39
Communication support worker 40
Dietician 40
Educational psychologist 40

General practitioner (GP) 40
Health visitor (Health Service) 40
Key worker 41
Learning disability nurses 41
Learning support assistant / teaching assistant 42
Named officer 42
Paediatric occupational therapist 42
Paediatrician (Health Service) 42
Paediatric neurologist 43
Physiotherapist 43
Portage home visitor 43
School nurse 43
Social worker (Childrens) 43
Special educational needs co-ordinator (SENCO) 44
Useful contacts 45

Ch.4 Finances-The Benefits System **53**
Right to maternity leave 53
Statutory Maternity Leave 56
Statutory Maternity Pay (SMP) 56
Early births or you lose your baby 56
If you're not eligible for SMP 57
How to claim 57
Proof you're pregnant 58
Maternity benefits 58
Extra leave 58
Parental leave 59
Your parenting leave entitlement 59

Special arrangements 60
Dealing with emergencies 60
Paternity leave and pay 61
What is paternity leave? 61
Taking paternity leave 61
Births 61
Adoptions and Surrogacy Arrangements 62
Receiving paternity pay 63
Statutory Paternity Pay 63
Contractual Paternity Pay 63
Other leave options 63
Annual leave 64
Unpaid time off 64
Attending Antenatal or Adoption Appointments 64
Still births and sick babies 65
Agency Workers and paternity rights 66
Employment rights during paternity leave 66
Entitlement to Parental Bereavement Leave and Pay 67
Who is entitled? 67
How can the leave and pay be taken? 68
Other benefits available if your child is disabled 68
Disability Living Allowance/Personal Independence Payment 68
Child Benefit 70
Carer's Allowance 73
Universal credit 80
Child tax credit 80
Disabled Facilities Grant 85

Housing Benefit and Council Tax Reduction 88
Family Fund 92
Help with health costs 93
Useful Contacts 98

Ch.5 Education **101**
Education and the law 101
Reasonable adjustments 102
Portage 102
Special Educational Needs (SEN) 103
Higher education 103
Children with special educational needs (SEN) 104
Support a child can receive 104
Extra help 105
Requesting an EHC assessment 105
Personal budgets 107
Independent support for children of all ages 107
Disabled people and financing studies 108
Students and means tested benefits 109
Useful contacts 111

Ch.6 Help With Transport and Equipment for You and Your Disabled Child **113**
Welfare benefits 113
The Blue Badge Scheme 114
The Motability Scheme 115
Use of Public Transport 118
Travel permits for buses and trains 118

Help with taxi fares 118
Community transport schemes 118
Equipment available for disabled children-Equipment - provision through local authorities & direct payments 119
Direct payments 119
Arranging an assessment 120
Wheelchairs 120
Other needs such as nappies and incontinence pads 121
Useful contacts 122

Ch.7 Holidays and Breaks for Disabled Children and Their Families 123
Respite breaks or short term breaks 124
Family Based Respite Care 124
Residential Respite Care 125
Play schemes and After School Clubs 126
Respite Care or Short-term Breaks in Your Home 126
Holidays 127
Useful contacts 128

Ch. 8 Disability and Employment 135
Entering employment 135
Jobcentre plus and Disability Employment Advisors 135
Work programmes 136
Community Work Placement Programme 136
Access to Work 137
Training 138
Benefits while training 139

When a person is in work 139
Disability and employers responsibilities 139
Reasonable adjustments in the workplace 140
Recruitment 142
Redundancy and retirement 143
Useful contacts 144

Index

****

Introduction

Many parents of disabled children find the experience of looking after that child all the more difficult and traumatic because of the lack of information from the professionals who work in the field of disability. In addition to the initial trauma of finding that their child has been diagnosed as disabled, if a diagnosis has been made at all, parents can be rendered powerless by a lack of information about their child's condition and the ongoing support that they need, plus knowledge of the services, support and benefits to which their child is entitled.

COVID 19 and disabled children

As we all know, the pandemic virtually shut the country, and all of its services, down, from March 2020 onwards. This created problems across the board in all sectors, not least those areas dealing with the provision of services to disabled children. Also, importantly, the mental and physical health of children, and particularly disabled children has suffered. At the time of writing, the country is pulling out of the pandemic and slowly returning to normal. However, it is necessary to take stock and to see what problems the last 16 months have created.

To this end the NSPCC have produced a report entitled **The impact of the coronavirus pandemic on child welfare: d/Deaf and disabled children- Publication date 2021.** The NSPCC used insight from Childline counselling sessions and contacts to the NSPCC helpline to highlight the impact of the coronavirus pandemic on children and young people.

The report focuses on what d/Deaf and disabled children are telling Childline, and what adults are telling the NSPCC helpline about d/Deaf and disabled children. This includes children who:

- are d/Deaf
- are on the autistic spectrum (in just over half of the Childline counselling sessions with disabled children between 1 April and 31 October 2020, children told us they are on the autism spectrum)
- have a condition such as attention deficit hyperactivity disorder (ADHD)
- have a learning disability
- have a physical disability such as cerebral palsy
- have visual impairment.

Key themes of the report include:

- worries about the pandemic
- coping with coronavirus restrictions
- learning during lockdown
- returning to school after lockdown
- family pressures
- children experiencing abuse
- getting support during the pandemic.

A Summary of Key findings of the report

- Coronavirus restrictions have caused disruption to young people's routines, which has been difficult for some children to cope with and adjust to.

- Support services have been harder for young people to access during the pandemic, with services either closed or severely reduced. Where services were transferred online, some young people found it difficult to access them, due to their disability.
- Home learning has also presented several challenges for some young people, including accessibility of online lessons and reduced additional support.
- Some young people have experienced delays in being assessed for support during the pandemic.
- After returning to school, some young people found they were no longer receiving the same level of support as they had been given before lockdown.
- The pandemic conditions have put additional stress on families where a child is disabled. Some parents have struggled to cope with the demands of caring for a disabled child with reduced support. Some children have also had to care for a disabled sibling during lockdown.
- Some young people report being unfairly, and in some cases aggressively, challenged for not wearing a face covering, even though they are exempt from doing so.

To read more about the findings from the report go to:

https://learning.nspcc.org.uk/research-resources/2021/coronavirus-insight-briefing-deaf-and-disabled-children.

The report highlights the enormous difficulties faced by disabled children and their parents. However, the question now is what to do to combat these difficulties. The Council for Disabled Children has updated its extremely useful guidance for disabled children and parents of disabled children. This particular site has a very wide range of easily accessible advice, covering all areas of concern for the parents of Disabled children. Go to:

https://councilfordisabledchildren.org.uk/help-resources/resources/covid-19-support-and-guidance.

A summary of the key areas of advice provided by the Council for Disabled Children is below. (In addition to advice for children and parents, there is advice for the professionals dealing with disabled children).

The CFDC offers the below advice and support:

- Education support for children and young people.
- Covid-19 Family Support Hub.
- SEND Summer Support Hub.
- WellChild - WellChild are offering a Direct Response Service to try and help families get the things they need including access to food delivery service and prescription collections.
- Contact - Coronavirus: Information for families with disabled children. Disabled Children's Partnership (DCP) - A wealth of resources for families, covering a

range of information, activities and condition specific advice

- Family Fund - A collection of links from organisations that provide services, advice and other help to families raising disabled or seriously ill children including information on vaccines.
- Challenging Behaviour Foundation (CBF) - Specific resources for the families of children, young people and adults with severe learning disabilities who display behaviours that challenge.
- Council for Disabled Children - Guidance and Advice on Coronavirus: Learning Disability and Autism Focus.
- Rehab Clinic Group - Student guide to managing mental health during COVID-19
- Limb Power - **Limb Power** have created online adaptive fitness sessions for children and young people with limb difference.
- Internet Matters - Internet Matters have launched a new website to help to support parents, carers, and young people with additional learning needs to stay safe online.
- Learning Resources to Support Home Schooling

It is hoped that his book, updated to ***2021,*** will greatly assist the parent(s) of a disabled child and also help to empower and point them in the right direction, enabling people to obtain the support and advice that is needed, both in the early years and later in life.

This book doesn't give information on specific disabilities. This information can be obtained from various sources, such as MENCAP and local libraries, which have a lot of information concerning organisations that exist to provide advice and support. A particularly good organisation is Contact a Family www.contact.org.uk which exists to help parents with disabled children and has a wealth of information. The book is aimed primarily at parent(s) but may be of interest to others such as professionals and agencies, and takes a very practical approach, dealing initially with a discussion of the early days, or months, after having a child diagnosed as disabled. The law and disability is then outlined, along with the professionals involved in the field of disability, and what they do and also the benefit system. Education is discussed, access to education and the responsibilities of local authorities. Holidays and breaks for disabled children and their parents are covered along with transport generally.

This book is a companion volume to A Straightforward Guide To The Rights of Disabled People, which covers the rights of adults who are disabled, either from birth or through accident. I hope it helps a great deal in your journey and makes life easier for both parent and child.

The book opens with a discussion of initial reactions and emotions of parents on learning that their child has a disability. This is a very important time and helps to set the book in context.

Doreen Jarrett

Chapter 1

The Early Days

When you have a child with a disability, you will have to cope with a number of issues. On one hand you will have to find your way through the maze of organisations that exist to help you as well as coping with your own emotions and the reactions of relatives and friends plus the reactions of siblings.

Some parents are given the news that their child has a disability at birth, or even before birth. Others might receive the diagnosis after months or years have elapsed. This very much depends on the particular condition. Depending on when you learn of a child's disability, your feelings will vary in reaction and also in intensity. These emotions will cover a whole range of feelings such as anger and disbelief, denial, frustration and guilt. Blame can be placed on oneself or one's partner, which is natural and should eventually pass as it can be rationalised over time. A certain amount of grief will be felt as, although you haven't lost the child you did not have the child that you expected. Ultimately, you will need to change the expectations that you had for him or her. Finally though, comes acceptance and the realisation that you need to live with the situation, love the child and give it the best that you can.

Depression is a common emotion, and can express itself through feelings of pessimism and hopelessness and lead to other difficulties such as problems with eating and sleeping. If you think that you are suffering from depression and recognise the signs then you will need to see your GP, and also in turn health visitors or other agencies.

As mentioned, for some parent's the actual diagnosis of a child's condition cannot be made until after a few years because certain things don't become evident until time has elapsed. This at least gives a parent time to adjust to what might be needed although it in no way diminishes the initial feelings of shock and anger.

Negative feelings towards the child

One of the emotions that you may find particularly difficult to deal with is that of harbouring negative feelings towards your child. The child may look different to others, although this is not always the case. It may take a time to develop a bond and love the child properly. This is perfectly normal and nothing to be ashamed of.

You may also feel over-protective which is a perfectly normal reaction. It can become problematic, however, if being over- protective prevents the child from attaining his or her own independence.

If you have feelings of wanting to harm your child then you will need to seek help immediately. Again, help can be obtained from various sources, such as your GP, health visitor or from a range of agencies detailed at the back of this book. Organisations such as Familylives, https://www.familylives.org.uk CRY-SIS https://www.cry-sis.org.uk and the NSPCC are particularly useful as they have a lot of experience in this area.

Coping with emotions

With time, and a lot of support, the vast majority of parent's do cope with their situation. They also grow to love their child and get a lot of pleasure from him or her. In the early days (months-years) the best way to cope with feelings that will inevitably arise from the discovery that your child has a disability is to be as open as possible and discuss your feelings with your partner, relatives and friends and also sympathetic professionals. As time goes by you will develop relations with professionals, those who you feel the most empathy with.

There are numerous groups dealing with all sorts of disabilities and they have networks of people who have been through the experience and can share their own experiences with you. You won't feel alone and can learn an awful lot.

It is also very important indeed to attempt to continue as normal a life as possible, going out to see friends for example. Doing the things that you enjoy and providing continuity in your own life is very important indeed and can provide balance.

Reactions of others in your life

Finally, in addition to coping yourself, you need to take into account the feelings of your own partner, if you have a partner or spouse, and ensure that you speak very openly and try to get along together on the same wavelength. Bottling up feelings is very unhealthy and can lead to problems. Relationships between parent's is one of the most important factors in how a family adjusts to disability and how family life develops.

If your partner is male and he is the father of the child, it is highly likely that he will experience the disability in a more negative way, in the first instance. Generally speaking, a mother will bond with a child more quickly than the father may and the father could experience feelings of rejection towards the child. Taking this into account, it is important that both parent's are fully involved with the child and its development right from the outset, sharing care, appointments with professionals and overall responsibility for development of the child.

Relatives can also exhibit differing emotions, such as guilt (for example, have they been indirectly responsible because of a genetic problem?). It might be that elder relatives, such as grandparents, have an old fashioned view of disability and may need updating with information about the child's condition.

Relatives might want to help in areas such as babysitting and doing housework, and this will involve them more and also take some of the pressure of you.

There is also the question of reactions of friends. Hopefully, your friends will react positively and want to help. It is important, once again, to be as open as possible. Allow them to see the baby as soon as possible which will reinforce the fact that the baby is a person rather than a disability. Friends can also offer practical support, particularly if they are good friends and are intelligent and sympathetic.

Reactions of siblings

If you have children, it is important to tell them about the child's disability as soon as possible. This goes without saying. How much you tell your children will depend on how old they are. Generally, children under a certain age, say 3 years old, are still too young to understand details about the disability or condition of their sibling. They can, however, be told that you are feeling sad and that their new baby sister or brother needs a lot of care and attention.

Older children can be told a little more about their sibling's disability. Use simple terms and try not to confuse them. Most children, older children, will understand. It is important to remember that you will still need to divide your time equally between children so as not to exclude them. Above all, try to involve sibling's in the child's development.

Coping with disability, and the reactions to disability, and the attendant emotions, is not easy. However, very importantly, try to remember that you are not alone and that there are numerous support groups out there with a network of people who are only to willing to offer support and share their experiences.

In the next chapter, we will look at how the law impacts on disability. Although this is a dry area, it is important to understand as it will give you an idea of your rights and the child's rights.

****

Useful Contacts

KIDS is a leading disabled children's charity that has been in existence for over 40 years working to enable disabled children and young people and their families www.kids.org.uk

Disability Rights (Main campaigning group)
Plexal
14 East Bay Lane
Here East
Queen Elizabeth Olympic Park
Stratford
London
E20 3BS
www.disabilityrightsuk.org
Email: enquiries@disabilityrightsuk.org
Office Number: 0330 995 0400
This line is not an advice line.

There are advice lines which can be accessed on the website

Child Disability help (general sites)
www.scope.org.uk/support/families/parents/help
www.gov.uk/help-for-disabled-chil

Contact a family (contact for families with disabled children)
209 City Road

London EC1V 1JN

0208 7608 8700

Helpline 0808 808 3555

www.contact.org.uk/

MENCAP (mental health charity)

The Royal MENCAP Society is a registered charity that offers services to children, young people and adults with learning disabilities. It offers help and advice on benefits, housing and employment. It also offers help and advice to anyone with any other issues, or will direct them to the right place. It can also provide information and support for leisure, recreational services (Gateway Clubs), residential services and holidays.

0808 808 1111

www.mencap.org

Familylives (support for families)

www.familylives.org.uk

0808 800 2222

CRY-SIS (helps with sleepless nights/support group)

www.cry-sis.org.uk

08451 228 669

****

Chapter 2

The Law and Disability

Although this book is specifically about the rights of disabled children, those rights sit within the wider body of law that covers all people with disabilities. Below is an outline of the law generally as it impacts on disability. This will help to set the scene and create a knowledge base from which you can develop your understanding.

The law and disability

In general, the wide body of laws that protect all people in the United Kingdom will apply to disabled people. Such laws can include consumer law, employment law and family law.

Later on in the book, in the chapter on education, we will be discussing The Children and Families Act 2014 Part 3: Children and young people with special educational needs and disabilities.

However, in certain important respects, the law that applies to disabled people, and gives an extra layer of protection is the Equality Act 2010. The rest of this chapter covers this Act.

This law is wide ranging and incorporated many previous Acts, such as the Disability Discrimination Act, and also clearly defines discrimination. Below is a summary of the Act.

However, as we go through the book continuous reference will be made to the Act as it applies to the many areas of life, such as employment and transport, that directly affects disabled people.

The Equality Act 2010

The Equality Act 2010 prohibits discrimination against people with the protected characteristics that are specified in section 4 of the Act. Disability is one of the specified protected characteristics. Protection from discrimination for disabled people applies to disabled people in a range of circumstances, covering the provision of goods, facilities and services, the exercise of public functions, premises, work, education, and associations. Only those people who are defined as disabled in accordance with section 6 of the Act, and the associated Schedules and regulations made under that section, will be entitled to the protection that the Act provides to disabled people. However, importantly, the Act also provides protection for non-disabled people who are subjected to direct discrimination or harassment because of their association with a disabled person or because they are wrongly perceived to be disabled.

The Act defines a disabled person as, simply, a person with a disability. A person has a disability for the purposes of the Act if he or she has a physical or mental impairment and the impairment has a substantial and long-term adverse effect on his or her ability to carry out normal day-to-day activities.

This means that, in general:

- the person must have an impairment that is either physical or mental
- the impairment must have adverse effects which are substantial
- the substantial adverse effects must be long-term and
- the long-term substantial adverse effects must have an effect on normal day-to-day activities

Definition of 'impairment'

The definition requires that the effects which a person may experience must arise from a physical or mental impairment. The term mental or physical impairment should be given its ordinary meaning. It is not necessary for the cause of the impairment to be established, nor does the impairment have to be the result of an illness. In many cases, there will be no dispute as to whether a person has an impairment. Any disagreement is more likely to be about whether the effects of the impairment are sufficient to fall within the definition and in particular whether they are long-term. This is a crucial fact.

Whether a person is disabled for the purposes of the Act is generally determined by reference to the effect that an impairment has on that person's ability to carry out normal day-to-day activities. An exception to this is a person with severe disfigurement. A disability can arise from a wide range of impairments which can be:

- sensory impairments, such as those affecting sight or hearing;

- impairments with fluctuating or recurring effects such as Rheumatoid arthritis, Myalgic encephalitis (ME), Chronic fatigue syndrome (CFS), Fibromyalgia, Depression and Epilepsy;
- progressive, such as Motor neurone disease, Muscular dystrophy, and forms of Dementia;
- auto-immune conditions such as Systemic lupus erythematosis (SLE);
- organ specific, including Respiratory conditions, such as Asthma, and cardiovascular diseases, including Thrombosis, Stroke and Heart disease;
- developmental, such as Autistic spectrum disorders (ASD), Dyslexia and Dyspraxia;
- learning disabilities;
- mental health conditions with symptoms such as anxiety, low mood, panic attacks, phobias, or unshared perceptions; eating disorders; bipolar affective disorders; obsessive compulsive disorders; personality disorders; post traumatic stress disorder, and some self-harming behaviour;
- Mental illnesses, such as depression and schizophrenia;
- produced by injury to the body, including to the brain.

Persons with HIV infection, cancer and multiple sclerosis

The Act states that a person who has cancer, HIV infection or Multiple sclerosis (MS) is a disabled person. This means that the person is protected by the Act effectively from the point of diagnosis.

Certain conditions are not regarded as impairments. These are:

- addiction to, or dependency on, alcohol, nicotine, or any other substance (other than in consequence of the substance being medically prescribed);
- the condition known as seasonal allergic rhinitis (e.g. hayfever), except where it aggravates the effect of another condition;
- tendency to set fires;
- tendency to steal;
- tendency to physical or sexual abuse of other persons;
- exhibitionism;

A person with an excluded condition may nevertheless be protected as a disabled person if he or she has an accompanying impairment which meets the requirements of the definition. For example, a person who is addicted to a substance such as alcohol may also have depression, or a physical impairment such as liver damage, arising from the alcohol addiction. While this person would not meet the definition simply on the basis of having an addiction, he or she may still meet the definition as a result of the effects of the depression or the liver damage.

Disfigurements which consist of a tattoo (which has not been removed), non-medical body piercing, or something attached through such piercing, are treated as not having a substantial adverse effect on the person's ability to carry out normal day-to-day activities.

The Act says that, except for the provisions in Part 12 (Transport) and section 190 (improvements to let dwelling houses), the provisions of the Act also apply in relation to a person who previously has had a disability as defined in the Act. This means that someone who is no longer disabled, but who met the requirements of the definition in the past, will still be covered by the Act. Also protected would be someone who continues to experience debilitating effects as a result of treatment for a past disability.

Definition of 'long-term effects'

The Act states that, for the purpose of deciding whether a person is disabled, a long-term effect of an impairment is one:

- which has lasted at least 12 months; or
- where the total period for which it lasts, from the time of the first onset, is likely to be at least 12 months; or
- which is likely to last for the rest of the life of the person affected

Special provisions apply when determining whether the effects of an impairment that has fluctuating or recurring effects are long-term. Also a person who is deemed to be a disabled person does not need to satisfy the long-term requirement.

The cumulative effect of related impairments should be taken into account when determining whether the person has experienced a long-term effect for the purposes of meeting the definition of a disabled person. The substantial adverse effect of an impairment which has developed from, or is likely to develop from, another impairment should be taken into account when determining whether the effect has lasted, or is likely to last at least twelve months, or for the rest of the life of the person affected.

Normal day-to-day activities

In general, day-to-day activities are things people do on a regular or daily basis, and examples include shopping, reading and writing, having a conversation or using the telephone, watching television, getting washed and dressed, preparing and eating food, carrying out household tasks, walking and travelling by various forms of transport, and taking part in social activities. Normal day-to-day activities can include general work-related activities, and study and education-related activities, such as interacting with colleagues, following instructions, using a computer, driving, carrying out interviews, preparing written documents, and keeping to a timetable or a shift pattern.

The term 'normal day-to-day activities' is not intended to include activities which are normal only for a particular person, or a small group of people. In deciding whether an activity is a normal day-to-day activity, account should be taken of how far it is carried out by people on a daily or frequent basis. In this context, 'normal' should be given its ordinary, everyday meaning.

A normal day-to-day activity is not necessarily one that is carried out by a majority of people. For example, it is possible that some activities might be carried out only, or more predominantly, by people of a particular gender, such as breast-feeding or applying make-up, and cannot therefore be said to be normal for most people. They would nevertheless be considered to be normal day-to-day activities.

Also, whether an activity is a normal day-to-day activity should not be determined by whether it is more normal for it to be carried out at a particular time of day. For example, getting out of bed and getting dressed are activities that are normally associated with the morning. They may be carried out much later in the day by workers who work night shifts, but they would still be considered to be normal day-to-day activities. The following examples demonstrate a range of day-to-day effects on impairment:

- Difficulty in getting dressed,
- Difficulty carrying out activities associated with toileting, or caused by frequent minor incontinence;
- Difficulty preparing a meal,
- Difficulty eating;
- Difficulty going out of doors unaccompanied, for example, because the person has a phobia, a physical restriction, or a learning disability;
- Difficulty waiting or queuing,

- Difficulty using transport; for example, because of physical restrictions, pain or fatigue, a frequent need for a lavatory or as a result of a mental impairment or learning disability;
- Difficulty in going up or down steps, stairs or gradients;
- A total inability to walk, or an ability to walk only a short distance without difficulty;
- Difficulty entering or staying in environments that the person perceives as strange or frightening;
- Behaviour which challenges people around the person, making it difficult for the person to be accepted in public places;
- Persistent difficulty crossing a road safely,
- Persistent general low motivation or loss of interest in everyday activities;
- Difficulty accessing and moving around buildings;
- Difficulty operating a computer, for example, because of physical restrictions in using a keyboard, a visual impairment or a learning disability;
- Difficulty picking up and carrying objects of moderate weight, such as a bag of shopping or a small piece of luggage, with one hand;
- Inability to converse, or give instructions orally, in the person's native spoken language;
- Difficulty understanding or following simple verbal instructions;

- Difficulty hearing and understanding another person speaking clearly over the voice telephone
- Persistent and significant difficulty in reading or understanding written material where this is in the person's native written language,
- Frequent confused behaviour, intrusive thoughts, feelings of being controlled, or delusions;
- Persistently wanting to avoid people or significant difficulty taking part in normal social interaction or forming social relationships,
- Persistent difficulty in recognising, or remembering the names of, familiar people such as family or friends;
- Persistent distractibility or difficulty concentrating;
- Compulsive activities or behaviour, or difficulty in adapting after a reasonable period to minor changes in a routine.

Whether a person satisfies the definition of a disabled person for the purposes of the Act will depend upon the full circumstances of the case. That is, whether the substantial adverse effect of the impairment on normal day-to-day activities is long term.

Specialised activities

Where activities are themselves highly specialised or involve highly specialised levels of attainment, they would not be regarded as normal day-to-day activities for most people. In some instances work-related activities are so highly specialised that they would not be regarded as normal day-to-day activities. The same is true of other specialised activities such as playing a musical instrument to a high standard of achievement; taking part in activities where very specific skills or level of ability are required; or playing a particular sport to a high level of ability, such as would be required for a professional footballer or athlete. Where activities involve highly specialised skills or levels of attainment, they would not be regarded as normal day-to-day activities for most people.

Normal day-to-day activities also include activities that are required to maintain personal well-being or to ensure personal safety, or the safety of other people. Account should be taken of whether the effects of an impairment have an impact on whether the person is inclined to carry out or neglect basic functions such as eating, drinking, sleeping, keeping warm or personal hygiene; or to exhibit behaviour which puts the person or other people at risk.

Indirect effects

An impairment may not directly prevent someone from carrying out one or more normal day-to-day activities, but it may still have a substantial adverse effect on how the person carries out those activities. For example pain or fatigue: where an impairment causes pain or fatigue, the person may have the ability to carry out a normal day-to-day activity, but may be restricted in the way that it is carried out because of experiencing pain in doing so. Or the impairment might make the activity more than usually fatiguing so that the person might not be able to repeat the task over a sustained period of time.

Disabled children

The effects of impairments may not be apparent in babies and young children because they are too young to have developed the ability to carry out activities that are normal for older children and adults. Regulations provide that an impairment to a child under six years old is to be treated as having a substantial and long-term adverse effect on the ability of that child to carry out normal day-to-day activities where it would normally have a substantial and long-term adverse effect on the ability of a person aged six years or over to carry out normal day-to-day activities.

Children aged six and older are subject to the normal requirements of the definition. That is, that they must have an impairment which has a substantial and long-term adverse effect on their ability to carry out normal day-to-day activities. However, in considering the ability of a child aged six or over to carry out a normal day-to-day activity, it is necessary to take account of the level of achievement which would be normal for a person of a similar age.

Part 6 of the Act provides protection for disabled pupils and students by preventing discrimination against them at school or in post-16 education because of, or for a reason related to, their disability. A pupil or student must satisfy the definition of disability as described in this guidance in order to be protected by Part 6 of the Act. The duties for schools in the Act, including the duty for schools to make reasonable adjustments for disabled children, are designed to dovetail with duties under the Special Educational Needs (SEN) framework which are based on a separate definition of special educational needs. Further information on these duties can be found in the SEN Code of Practice and the Equality and Human Rights Commission's Codes of Practice.

For more advice and guidance on the law and disabled children you can obtain Disabled Children: A Legal Handbook 3rd edition, free from the Council for Disabled Children:

https://councilfordisabledchildren.org.uk/help-resources/resources/disabled-children-legal-handbook-3rd-edition

****

Useful Contacts

Gov.uk

www.gov.uk/rights-disabled-person/overview

Children's Legal Centre (Head Office)

Coram Children's Legal Centre

Wellington House

4th Floor, 90-92 Butt Road

Colchester

Essex

CO3 3DA.

Tel: 01206 714 650 (*for general queries only, they cannot give legal advice or a referral through this number*)

E-mail: info@coramclc.org.uk

London Office

Coram Children's Legal Centre

Coram Campus

41 Brunswick Square

LONDON

WC1N 1AZ

Tel: 020 7713 0089 (*for general queries only, they cannot give legal advice or a referral through this number*)

Disability Law Service

39-45 Cavell Street

The Foundry
17 Oval way, London, SE11 5RR
0207 791 9800
www.dls.org.uk

Disability Rights Commission
Telephone: 08457 622 633
Textphone: 08457 622 644
You can speak to an operator at any time between 8am and 8pm, Monday to Friday.

Post: DRC Helpline
FREEPOST MID02164
Stratford upon Avon
CV37 9BR

Disability Rights UK
14 East Bay Lane
Here East
Queen Elizabeth Olympic Park
Stratford
London
E20 3BS
www.disabilityrightsuk.org
Office Number: 0330 995 0400
This line is not an advice line.

There are advice lines which can be accessed on the website

Chapter 3

Professionals and Organisations That You and Your Child Might be Involved With

---

When you have a disabled child, you will inevitably come into contact with a variety of different professionals from health services, social services, education and different voluntary organisations. This will continue throughout your son or daughter's childhood and early adulthood, sometimes throughout his or her life.

This can be overwhelming and in the first instance you may be confused about each persons role, how they can help you and who employs them. This chapter outlines the different roles that professionals play and how they can help you. In addition, there are a number of agencies listed where you can get all the advice and support that you need. Some of these agencies are statutory, which are the ones run by the state under legislation, such as the NHS, and some are voluntary. The one common denominator is that they all provide invaluable help and support.

Clinical psychologist

A clinical psychologist is a health professional who helps people with specific problems with learning or behaviour difficulties.

Communication support worker

A communication support worker works alongside teachers to provide sign language support for young deaf children in nursery or school.

Dietician

A dietician is a health professional who gives advice about nutrition and swallowing or feeding difficulties.

Educational psychologist

An educational psychologist is qualified teacher who is also trained as a psychologist. They help children who find it difficult to learn or to understand or communicate with others. They can assess your child's development and provide support and advice.

General practitioner (GP)

A GP is a family doctor who works in a surgery either on their own or with other GPs. Your doctor deals with your child's general health and can refer you to clinics, hospitals and specialists when needed.

Health visitor (Health Service)

A health visitor is a registered nurse or a midwife with additional training. They visit families at home to give help, advice and practical assistance about the care of very young children. Some areas have specialist health visitors who have particular experience and expertise supporting families with a young disabled child.

Key worker

Some families have a key worker. A key worker will see you regularly and make sure you have all the information you need. They will also make sure that services from all the different areas, including health, education and social services, are well co-ordinated. Key workers can act as a central point of contact for professionals working with your family, and make sure information about your child is shared where necessary.

'Designated' and 'non-designated' key workers

A 'non-designated' key worker is someone who is already working with a family, in another role. They take on the responsibilities of a key worker in addition to any other help or therapy they provide for the child or parents. 'Designated' key workers are employed mainly to co-ordinate information and support for families.

Learning disability nurses

Learning disability nurses are specialist nurses who work with children and adults with a learning disability and with their families. They can help you find services for your child.

Learning support assistant / teaching assistant

A learning support assistant or teaching assistant is someone who works alongside teachers. They support individual children or small groups to help them learn and take part in activities in schools or nurseries.

Named officer

A named officer is your family's contact person at the local education authority, if it issues a statement of special educational needs for your child. They manage your child's statutory assessment and write up the statement of needs.

Paediatric occupational therapist

A paediatric occupational therapist helps children with difficulties in carrying out the activities of everyday life, such as sitting in a chair, holding a spoon and fork or drinking from a cup. They carry out assessments to see if your child would benefit from using specialist equipment like adapted cups, buggies or chairs. They can also advise you on lifting and handling your child safely.

Paediatrician (Health Service)

A paediatrician is a doctor who specialises in working with babies and children. They are often the first point of contact for families who find out their child has an impairment or medical condition. Paediatricians may give you a diagnosis about your child's condition, answer any questions you may have and refer you to specialist services.

Paediatric neurologist

A paediatric neurologist is a doctor who specialises in how the brain works in very young children.

Physiotherapist

A physiotherapist is a health professional who specialises in physical and motor development. They can assess your child and develop a plan that might include helping your child control their head movement, sit, crawl or walk. A physiotherapist may see your child at home or in other settings, like a nursery.

Portage home visitor

An eucational professional who can come to the home of pre-school children with special educational needs and their families. Portage home visitors can come from a range of professional backgrounds. They may be teachers, therapists, nursery nurses, health visitors or volunteers with relevant experience.

School nurse

A school nurse is a medical nurse, based in a school, who provides support for children's medical needs.

Social worker (Childrens)

A social worker is a professional who provides practical help and advice about counselling, transport, home help and other services. They are normally employed by the local council. Social workers may also be able to help you with claiming benefits or getting equipment you need at home.

Special educational needs co-ordinator (SENCO)

SENCOs are members of staff at a nursery, playgroup or school who co-ordinate special educational needs activities and services. They make sure that children who have special educational needs receive appropriate support.

****

Useful contacts

Support organisations

There are numerous support organisations that exist to help parents with disabled children. The internet has many useful sites which can direct you to specific organisations. One particularly good site is:

http://www.accessiblecountryside.org.uk/organisations. They have a comprehensive list of professionals which is very helpful and detailed. Below are listed a few more such organisations.

Cerebra

A unique charity set up to help improve the lives of children and young people with brain-related conditions through researching, educating and directly supporting children and their carers.

Cerebra
The MacGregor Office
Jolly Tar Lane
Carmarthen
SA31 3LW
Helpline (freephone): 0800 328 1159
Telephone: +44 (0) 1267 244200
Email: enquiries@cerebra.org.uk

Citizens Advice Bureau

Helps people resolve their legal, money and other problems by providing free, confidential and impartial information and advice. It has a number of field offices across England. Myddelton House,

Citizens Advice,
3rd Floor North,
200 Aldersgate, London,
EC1A 4HD
www.citizensadvice.org.uk (local offices)
www.adviceguide.org.uk

Contact a Family

A UK-wide charity providing support, advice and information for families with children with additional needs. It runs a helpline for family members and can help you get in touch with other parents of disabled children living near you. Will divert calls to Scotland, Northern Ireland and Wales as appropriate
www.contact.org.uk
0808 8083555

Council for Disabled Children

A national forum for the discussion, development and dissemination of a wide range of policy and practice issues relating to service provision for children and young people with disabilities and special educational needs. Membership is drawn from a wide range of professional, voluntary and statutory organisations and includes parent representatives and representatives of disabled people.

www.councilfordisabledchildren.org.uk

Family and Childcare Trust

A national childcare charity working to promote high-quality, affordable childcare for everyone. It provides information about all aspects of childcare.

www.familyandchildcaretrust.org

020 7239 7535

Department for Education

The Department for Education is responsible for education and children's services in England. They work to achieve a highly educated society in which opportunity is equal for children and young people, no matter what their background or family circumstances. DfE is a ministerial department, supported by 9 agencies and public bodies.

https://www.gov.uk/government/organisations/department-for-education

0370 000 2288

Disability Rights UK

Plexal

14 East Bay Lane

Here East

Queen Elizabeth Olympic Park
Stratford
London
E20 3BS
www.disabilityrightsuk.org
Office Number: 0330 995 0400
This line is not an advice line.

There are advice lines which can be accessed on the website

Family Information Service (FIS)

The FIS can give you information about the full range of childcare and other services for children, young people and families available in the area. You can contact the FIS through your local authority office or find you local FIS contact details at the following website.

Information Advice and Support Services Network (IASSN)

The Information, Advice and Support Services Network (IASS Network) provide training and support to local Information Advice and Support (IAS) Services across England. The IASS Network was previously known as the National Parent Partnership Network (NPPN), who undertook a similar role with local Parent Partnership Services.
www.councilfordisabledchildren.org.uk

Mencap

The Royal MENCAP Society is a registered charity that offers services to children, young people and adults with learning disabilities. It offers help and advice on benefits, housing and employment. It also offers help and advice to anyone with any other issues, or will direct them to the right place. It can also provide information and support for leisure, recreational services (Gateway Clubs), residential services and holidays.

www.mencap.org.uk
help@mencap.org.uk
0808 8081111

NHS Direct

A 24-hour nurse advice and health information service, providing confidential information on what to do if you or a family member is feeling ill, have particular health conditions, or need local healthcare services or self-help and support organisations.

www.nhsdirect.nhs.uk
0300 311 22 33
Email: england.contactus@nhs.net

The Royal National Institute of Blind People (RNIB)

RNIB is the leading charity offering information, support and advice to almost two million people with sight loss. It has practical ways to help those living with sight loss, including advice about travelling, shopping, managing money and finances, and technology for blind and partially sighted people.

105 Judd Street
London
WC1H 9NE
www.rnib.org.uk
helpline@rnib.org.uk

Scope

Scope is the UK's leading disability charity. Its focus is on children, young people and adults with cerebral palsy and people living with other severe and complex impairments. Its vision is a world where disabled people have the same opportunities to fulfill their life ambitions as non-disabled people.
www.scope.org.uk
0808 800 3333

Sense

The major UK voluntary organisation for children, young people and adults born with multi- sensory impairment (MSI) and their families. The website has information about the help and services available to people with MSI, their families and professionals.
101 Pentonville Road
London N1 9LG
www.sense.org.uk
info@sense.org.uk
0300 330 9256

Transition Information Network (TIN)

The network is hosted by the Council for Disabled Children. The aim of the website is to provide information to parents and practitioners about disabled young people's transition to adulthood. There is also a young people's section with information, news and events.

43 Fore Street,
Totnes,
TQ9 5HN,
UK
www.transitioninfonetwork.org.uk

Telephone: +44 (0)1803 865 669

****

Chapter 4

Finances-The Benefits System

Having looked at the role of the professional, in this chapter we will look at the rights of the disabled child and the rights of their parents/carers in relation to the benefit system. There are many benefits available which might be relevant to parents of disabled children. Here we cover the main benefits. For the whole range of welfare benefits that a person may be entitled to for the period 2021/2022 go to:
https://www.gov.uk/government/publications/benefit-and-pension-rates-2021-to-2022/benefit-and-pension-rates-2021-to-2022

For the purposes of this chapter we will start with the period of pregnancy. Pregnancy and maternity is one of the protected characteristics in the Equality Act 2010 and there is implied into every woman's term of employment a maternity equality clause (s 73 Equality Act 2010). The Act protects women from direct discrimination (s 13(1)) and indirect discrimination (s 19(1)) in relation to pregnancy and maternity.

Right to maternity leave

When you take time off to have a baby you might be eligible for:

- Statutory Maternity Leave
- Statutory Maternity Pay
- paid time off for antenatal care
- extra help from the government

You may also be eligible to get Shared Parental Leave and Pay.

Employment rights when on leave

Your employment rights are protected while on Statutory Maternity Leave. This includes your right to:

- pay rises
- build up (accrue) holiday
- return to work

Leave

Statutory Maternity Leave is 52 weeks. It's made up of:

- Ordinary Maternity Leave - first 26 weeks
- Additional Maternity Leave - last 26 weeks

You don't have to take 52 weeks but you must take 2 weeks' leave after your baby is born (or 4 weeks if you work in a factory). You may be entitled to take some of your leave as Shared Parental Leave.

Start date and early births

Usually, the earliest you can start your leave is 11 weeks before the expected week of childbirth. Leave will also start:

- the day after the birth if the baby is early
- automatically if you're off work for a pregnancy-related illness in the 4 weeks before the week (Sunday to Saturday) that your baby is due

Change your date for returning to work

You must give your employer at least 8 weeks' notice if you want to change your return to work date.

Pay

Statutory Maternity Pay (SMP) is paid for up to 39 weeks. You get:

- 90% of your average weekly earnings (before tax) for the first 6 weeks £151.97 (2021) then 90% of your average weekly earnings (whichever is lower) for the next 33 weeks

SMP is paid in the same way as your wages (for example monthly or weekly). Tax and National Insurance will be deducted.

If you take Shared Parental Leave you'll get Statutory Shared Parental Pay (ShPP). ShPP is £151.97 a week or 90% of your average weekly earnings, whichever is lower.

Start date

SMP usually starts when you take your maternity leave. It starts automatically if you're off work for a pregnancy-related illness in the 4 weeks before the week (Sunday to Saturday) that your baby is due.

Statutory Maternity Leave

You qualify for Statutory Maternity Leave if:

- you're an employee not a 'worker'
- you give your employer the correct notice

It doesn't matter how long you've been with your employer, how many hours you work or how much you get paid.

You can't get Statutory Maternity Leave if you have a child through surrogacy - you could get Statutory Adoption Leave and Pay instead.

Statutory Maternity Pay (SMP)

To qualify for SMP you must:

- earn on average at least £120 a week (2021/2)
- give the correct notice
- give proof you're pregnant
- have worked for your employer continuously for at least 26 weeks continuing into the 'qualifying week' - the 15th week before the expected week of childbirth

You can't get SMP if you go into police custody during your maternity pay period. It won't restart when you're discharged.

Early births or you lose your baby

You can still get Statutory Maternity Leave and SMP if your baby:

- is born early

- is stillborn after the start of your 24th week of pregnancy
- dies after being born

If you're not eligible for SMP

Your employer must give you form SMP1 explaining why you can't get SMP within 7 days of making their decision. You may be eligible for Maternity Allowance instead.

How to claim

Statutory Maternity Leave

At least 15 weeks before your due date, tell your employer when the baby is due and when you want to start your maternity leave. Your employer can ask for this in writing.

Your employer must write to you within 28 days confirming your start and end dates.

Statutory Maternity Pay (SMP)

Tell your employer you want to stop work to have a baby and the day you want your SMP to start. You must give them at least 28 days' notice (in writing if they ask for it) and proof that you're pregnant. Your employer must confirm within 28 days how much SMP you'll get and when it will start and stop. If they decide you're not eligible, they must give you form SMP1 within 7 days of making their decision and explain why.

Proof you're pregnant

You need to give your employer proof of the pregnancy to get SMP. You don't need it for maternity leave. Within 21 days of your SMP start date (or as soon as possible if the baby's born early) give your employer either:

- a letter from your doctor or midwife
- your MATB1 certificate - doctors and midwives will give you this no more than 20 weeks before the due date

You won't get SMP if you don't give your employer proof that the baby is due.

Maternity benefits

Working Tax Credit - this can continue for 39 weeks after you go on maternity leave

Income Support - you may get this while you're not working

You could get a £500 Sure Start Maternity Grant (usually if it's your first child).

If you're not eligible for Statutory Maternity Pay, you could get Maternity Allowance from the government.

Company maternity schemes

You might get more than the statutory amount of leave and pay if your employer has a company maternity scheme. They can't offer you less than the statutory amount.

Extra leave

You could get 18 weeks' unpaid parental leave after the birth - this may be restricted to 4 weeks per year.

Parental leave

Parental leave is a legal right to take time off from work to look after a child or make arrangements for a child's welfare. Employers are not legally required to pay workers taking parental leave, so many do not. However, if you are on a low income, you may qualify for income support while you are on parental leave.

Mothers and fathers qualify for statutory parental leave whether they are biological or adoptive parents.

Parental leave is different to other parenting-related leave arrangements such as maternity, adoption and paternity leave.

Your parenting leave entitlement

Working parents are entitled to take up to 18 weeks' parental leave per child up to their eighteenth birthday. Parental leave can be taken for any reason as long as it's related to the care of your child. Examples of the way it might be used include:

- spending more time with your child in their early years;
- accompanying your child during a stay in hospital;
- looking at new schools;
- settling your child into new childcare arrangements;
- enabling your family to spend more time together. For example, taking them to stay with grandparents.

If you take less than four weeks' parental leave in one block, you have the legal right to return to your old job. If you take more than four weeks in a block, you are only entitled to return to the job you did before if it is reasonably practicable. If it isn't, your employer must give you a comparable and appropriate job.

You can only take parental leave if you have been continuously employed for not less than a year and have, or expect to have responsibility for the child. "Responsibility for the child" is a legal term. You will normally have responsibility for the child if you are the mother of the child or the father of the child and you are either married to the mother of the child or your name appears on the birth certificate of the child, having registered jointly with the mother.

Special arrangements

Some employers allow flexibility in the way parental leave is taken. You might, therefore, be able to work reduced hours over a given period, for example, without losing any pay. Or your employer may allow you parental leave even though your child is over the statutory age for you to legally qualify.

Dealing with emergencies

Even if you don't qualify for parental leave, you should be able to get time off to deal with genuine emergencies. You have the right to take a reasonable amount of unpaid time off to deal with certain emergencies involving people you care for. You qualify for "time off for dependents" regardless of how long you have been working for your employer.

Paternity leave and pay

Employees whose partner is having a baby, adopting a child or having a baby through a surrogacy arrangement may be entitled to paternity leave and pay. Workers, while not entitled to paternity leave, may be entitled to receive paternity pay.

What is paternity leave?

Paternity leave is a period of either one or two consecutive weeks that fathers or partners can take off from work to care for their baby or child. It is available to employees who:

- have or expect to have responsibility for the child's upbringing
- are the biological father of the child, the mother's husband or partner (including same sex relationships) **or** the partner of the primary adopter
- have worked continuously for their employer for 26 weeks ending with the 15th week before the baby is due, or the end of the week in which the child's adopter is notified of being matched with the child (UK adoption), or the date the child enters the UK (overseas adoptions).

Taking paternity leave

Births

An employee must inform their employer no later than the end of the 15th week before the expected week of childbirth that they wish to take paternity leave. They should say when the baby is due, if they're going to take one or two weeks off, and when they expect their paternity leave to start.

An employee can choose for their leave to begin on:

- the day the baby is born
- a certain number of days after the baby is born
- a specific date which is not earlier than when the baby is due.

Paternity leave cannot start before the baby is born and the baby may not arrive on time. An employer should therefore be prepared to be flexible with cover arrangements for employees planning to take paternity leave.

Employees will need to complete their paternity leave within 56 days of the actual date of birth of the child.

Adoptions and Surrogacy Arrangements

When adopting, one partner, if they qualify, can take adoption leave as the main adopter and the other may be entitled to paternity leave. A period of paternity leave when adopting a child can start:

- on the date of placement
- an agreed number of days after the date of placement
- on the date the child arrives in the UK or an agreed number of days after (for overseas adoption)
- the day the child is born or the day after for surrogate parents.

In all adoptions, an employee will need to have taken their Paternity Leave within 56 days of the placement date.

Receiving paternity pay

Employees or workers who take time off may be entitled to either Statutory Paternity Pay or Contractual Paternity Pay.

Statutory Paternity Pay

Statutory Paternity Pay will be payable if an employee or worker has been:

- working continuously for one company for at least 26 weeks ending with the 15th week before the expected week of childbirth
- has an average weekly earnings at least equal to the lower earnings limit for National Insurance contributions.

The rate for 2021/22 is £151.97 per week or 90 per cent of the average weekly earnings, whichever is less.

Contractual Paternity Pay

An employer may choose to offer a rate of pay which is higher than the statutory rate. The amount and the length for which it is paid should be set out in the terms and conditions of employment. Contractual paternity pay cannot be lower than the statutory rate.

Other leave options

An employee may not qualify for paternity leave, or they may want to take some additional time off when the baby is born. In these circumstances an employee could consider the following:

Shared Parental Leave

This gives parents more flexibility in how they share the care of their child in the first year following birth or adoption. Eligible parents can exchange part of their maternity or adoption leave for Shared Parental Leave. They can then share this leave with each other in a way that best suit their needs in caring for their child.

Annual leave

An employee could submit an annual leave request to take time off at the time the baby is born. This should be done in accordance with the employer's annual leave policy and the employer would have the right to accept or decline the request depending on business needs.

Unpaid time off

An employee could discuss with their employer whether they could come to an agreement to take unpaid time off. This could only be done if both employee and employer agree to it.

Attending Antenatal or Adoption Appointments

Antenatal classes

Fathers and partners of a pregnant woman are entitled to unpaid time off during working hours to accompany her to two ante-natal appointments. The time off should not exceed 6.5 hours per appointment and should be used to travel to and attend the appointment. If this takes less than 6.5 hours the employee should return to work unless alternative arrangements have been made with their employer.

There is no legal right to paid time off for attending antenatal appointments. However, an employee's contract of employment may entitle them to the time off with pay. If an employee does not want to take unpaid time off, they could request annual leave or ask if they could work the hours at a different time. The right to two unpaid antenatal appointments also includes employees who will become parents through a surrogacy arrangement if they expect to satisfy the conditions for, and intend to apply for, a Parental Order.

Adoption appointments

The main adopter is able to take paid time off for up to 5 adoption appointments. The main adopter's partner (secondary adopter) is entitled to take unpaid time off for up to 2 appointments.

Still births and sick babies

If the baby is stillborn after the twenty fourth week of pregnancy or if the baby is born alive at any point (even if the baby later passes away) the employee is entitled to full paternity rights if they satisfy the conditions above.

When a baby is born prematurely or with health needs an employee may not want to be thinking about work. An employer should offer appropriate support in these circumstances.

Agency Workers and paternity rights

Agency workers do not usually qualify for paternity leave (unless they are an employee of the agency). However, an agency worker may qualify for paternity pay if they meet the qualifying criteria. If an agency worker qualifies for paternity pay they should write to their agency at least 28 days before they want the payment to begin stating:

- the agency worker's name
- when the baby is due
- when the worker would like the payment to begin
- whether they are requesting one or two weeks pay.

Agency workers can usually choose when to make themselves available for work so may choose to be unavailable for work for a period of time after the baby is born. An agency worker whose partner is pregnant has the right to attend two unpaid antenatal appointments with their partner once they have completed a twelve week qualifying period with one hiring company.

Employment rights during paternity leave

An employee has the right to not be treated less favourably by their employer for taking, or proposing to take, paternity leave. An employee also has the right to return to their own job following a period of paternity leave and their terms and conditions should remain the same.

Annual leave (including Bank Holidays where applicable) continues to accrue during paternity leave and an employee must be able to take this leave at some point during their leave year.

New entitlement to Parental Bereavement Leave and Pay

The Government has introduced a new workplace right to Parental Bereavement Leave and Pay for parents who lose a child under the age of 18, including those who suffer a stillbirth from 24 weeks of pregnancy. The Parental Bereavement (Leave and Pay) Act gained Royal Assent in September 2018 and came into force on April 2020.

Who will be entitled?

Employed parents who lose a child under the age of 18 (or those who suffer stillbirth from 24 weeks) will be entitled to 2 weeks of Parental Bereavement Leave as a 'day-one' right. Those with at least 26 weeks continuous service at the date of their child's death and earnings above the Lower Earnings Limit will also be entitled to Parental Bereavement Pay, paid at the statutory flat weekly rate of £151.97 (or 90% of average earnings, where this is lower).

The definition of a 'bereaved parent' is guided by the principle that those who are the 'primary carers' of the child should be the focus of the entitlement. The entitlement will apply to the child's 'legal' parents; individuals with a court order to give them day-to-day responsibility for caring for the child; and primary carers who do not have legal status, such as kinship carers. In all cases, eligibility will be based on facts that will be clear to both the employee and their employer in order to minimise confusion.

How can the leave and pay be taken?

Eligible parents will be able to take both the leave and pay as either a single block or one or two weeks, or as two separate blocks of one week of leave and/or pay (taken at different times). The employee will have 56 weeks from the date of their child's death in which to take the entitlement so as to allow parents to take the leave (and pay) at important moments, such as anniversaries, if they wish.

Other benefits available if your child is disabled

Disability Living Allowance and Personal Independence Payment

If you have a disabled child under 16, you may be able to claim Disability Living Allowance (DLA) for them. DLA has two components. The mobility component may be paid if your child has problems with getting around, and the care component may be paid if they have care needs which are more than most children of their age.

You cannot get the mobility component for a child under three. There is no age requirement for the care component, but you cannot usually claim it for a baby under three months old. This is because your child must have had care needs or mobility problems for at least three months before they can be entitled to DLA, unless they are terminally ill. It can be difficult to claim DLA for a young child and it may help to get specialist advice.

If your child is 16 or over and on DLA, they will be invited to claim Personal Independence Payment (PIP) instead of DLA, unless they are terminally ill (when they stay on DLA until their award expires). There is more information about the transition to PIP on the Contact website https://contact.org.uk (it's well worth looking at this website for information on the rights of families with disabled children). Contact also has skilled advisors to help you work out what benefits you may be entitled to across the board. the site also deals with Scotland and Northern Ireland.

If your child is 16 or over and doesn't have an existing DLA claim, they will have to claim PIP.

DLA and PIP, claimed for you or your children, do not depend on income so are not affected when you move into or out of paid work.

DLA and PIP are complex benefits. It is advisable to seek personal advice when applying because the claim forms are long and you are more likely to be successful with professional advice. Whilst your child is under 16, you claim for them as an appointee. When they reach 16, they can claim in their own right or if appropriate, you can continue to be an appointee, but don't assume this happens automatically as you may need to show why they are unable to act as the claimant themselves.

DLA and PIP are 'passports' to other benefits and services – for example, you may get more Universal Credit (see below) if your child receives DLA or PIP.

Contact can help you with any questions you have about benefits for a disabled child. Your local Citizens Advice may be able to help fill in forms, or there may be a local disabled persons' or carers' organisation which can help. Scope may be able to help you find organisations local to you who can help with claim forms.

The lowest DLA child rates 2021 start at £23.70 and the highest rate is £152.15 a week. The amount you get depends on the level of help needed for the child. Note: In most cases, the child will get an assessment to determine what kind of help will be most appropriate.

Personal Independence Payment (PIP) is made up of 2 parts - a daily living part and a mobility part. Whether you get one or both of these and how much you'll get depends on how severely your condition affects you.

The weekly rate for the daily living part of PIP is either £60.00 or £89.60. The weekly rate for the mobility part of PIP is either £23.70 or £62.55.

Child Benefit

You should also be able to claim Child Benefit. You don't get extra Child Benefit for a disabled child but you may be entitled to additional amounts of other benefits if your child gets DLA or PIP. You get Child Benefit if you're responsible for bringing up a child who is:

- under 16
- under 20 if they stay in approved education or training

Only one person can get Child Benefit for a child. It's paid every 4 weeks and there's no limit to how many children you can claim for.

If you or your partner earn over £50,000

You may have to pay back some of your Child Benefit in tax if your (or your partner's) individual income is over £50,000.

What you'll get

There are 2 Child Benefit rates. (2021/22)

Who the allowance is for	Rate (weekly)
Eldest or only child	£21.15
Additional children	£14 per child

If your child is over 16, they will have to meet additional conditions for you to carry on getting Child Benefit, to do with being in full-time education. The rules are the same as for children who are not disabled; if your child leaves full-time education, you may no longer be entitled to Child Benefit for them.

You can't get Child Benefit for a young person who claims Universal Credit (see below). If you are not sure whether a young person should claim UC or it would be better to continue to claim for them, get advice. You should claim Child Benefit if:

- You are responsible for a child under 16.
- Or you are responsible for a young person aged 16-19 in certain circumstances.

Being responsible for a child normally means that the child lives with you. The person responsible for the child does not have to be the parent, but only one person can claim Child Benefit for one child at the same time.

If you share care of a child or young person with somebody else, you may need advice about what will happen to Child Benefit. You may be able to decide between you who will make the claim, or if you make competing claims, HMRC will decide, using priority rules to help them do so. You can have an arrangement where different people claim Child Benefit for different children (if you have responsibility for more than one child shared with another person), or one person claims Child Benefit and another person claims Child Tax Credit.

You cannot usually claim Child Benefit if your child is in the care of the local authority. You can get information about this from the Family Rights Group, or seek further advice.

In some cases, you can get Child Benefit if you contribute to the cost of supporting a child, but this will usually only apply if no one else is claiming. You should get advice if you think this applies to you.

Carers allowance

If you care for a disabled person, you may be able to claim Carer's Allowance, and in some cases, Universal Credit. Even if you are working and earn too much to get Carer's Allowance, you may still be able to get Universal Credit. It can include a carer element (which increases the amount you can get) if you meet certain conditions.

You may be eligible for Carer's Allowance if you, the person you care for and the type of care you provide meets certain criteria.

The person you care for

The person you care for must already get one of these benefits:

- Personal Independence Payment - daily living component
- Disability Living Allowance - the middle or highest care rate
- Attendance Allowance

- Constant Attendance Allowance at or above the normal maximum rate with an Industrial Injuries Disablement Benefit
- Constant Attendance Allowance at the basic (full day) rate with a War Disablement Pension
- Armed Forces Independence Payment
- Child Disability Payment - the middle or highest care rate

If someone else also cares for the same person as you, only one of you can claim Carer's Allowance.

The type of care you provide

You need to spend at least 35 hours a week caring for someone. This can include:

- helping with washing and cooking
- taking the person you care for to a doctor's appointment
- helping with household tasks, like managing bills and shopping

If you or the person you care for are affected by coronavirus, you can still claim Carer's Allowance if you provide care remotely. This includes giving emotional support over the phone or online.

Your eligibility

All of the following must apply:

- you're 16 or over
- you spend at least 35 hours a week caring for someone

- you've been in England, Scotland or Wales for at least 2 of the last 3 years (this does not apply if you're a refugee or have humanitarian protection status)
- you normally live in England, Scotland or Wales, or you live abroad as a member of the armed forces (you might still be eligible if you're moving to or already living in an EEA country or Switzerland)
- you're not in full-time education
- you're not studying for 21 hours a week or more
- you're not subject to immigration control
- your earnings are £128 or less a week after tax, National Insurance and expenses
- If your earnings are sometimes more than £128 a week you might still be eligible for Carer's Allowance. Your average earnings may be calculated to work out if you're eligible.

Calculating your earnings

Your earnings are any income from employment and self-employment after tax, National Insurance and expenses. Expenses can include:

- 50% of your pension contributions
- equipment you need to do your job, for example specialist clothing
- travel costs between different workplaces that are not paid for by your employer, for example fuel or train fares
- business costs if you're self-employed, for example a computer you only use for work

If you pay a carer to look after the disabled person or your children while you work, you can treat care costs that are less than or equal to 50% of your earnings as an expense. The carer must not be your spouse, partner, parent, child or sibling.

Payments that do not count as earnings include:

- money received from an occupational or private pension
- contributions towards your living or accommodation costs from someone you live with (they cannot be a tenant or boarder)
- the first £20 a week and 50% of the rest of any income you make from someone boarding in your home
- a loan or advance payment from your employer

If you get State Pension

You cannot get the full amount of both Carer's Allowance and your State Pension at the same time. If your pension is £67.60 a week or more, you will not get a Carer's Allowance payment. If your pension is less than £67.60 a week, you'll get a Carer's Allowance payment to make up the difference.

If you get Pension Credit

If your State Pension is more than £67.60 a week (the equivalent of carers allowance), you will not get a Carer's Allowance payment but your Pension Credit payments will increase instead.

If you're not eligible

You might be eligible for Carer's Credit if you're not eligible for Carer's Allowance.

Universal credit

If you are on a low income and you are not already claiming Income Support, income-based Jobseeker's Allowance, income-related Employment and Support Allowance, Housing Benefit or tax credits, you could consider claiming Universal Credit (UC). This is a benefit which will replace those benefits and so if you claim it, they will usually stop. You could end up worse off, so always seek advice. However, if you are not claiming these benefits, UC may be worth claiming. It can include extra amounts for a disabled child who is on DLA or PIP, called a disabled child element.

Over 16s who are not working and would have difficulty working because of illness or disability can claim Universal Credit themselves. However, you can't claim Child Benefit, or a child element or disabled child element in Child Tax Credit or Universal Credit, in respect of a young person at the same time as they claim UC, so you may need advice about which to claim, or you can research the amounts involved.

You can look at the different benefit amounts which would be paid depending on who claims by using an online calculator like the one on the website Turn2Us. Even if your young person claims UC, you can still be their appointee for the benefit, if that is necessary (that means you would be responsible for making the claim and reporting all changes of circumstances).

When your child first claims UC, they will need to submit a medical certificate (evidence that they are not fit for work) and be referred to a work capability assessment. If they are found to have limited capability for work or limited capability for work-related activity they can continue to get UC whilst under 18. If they are found capable of work, it's worth seeking advice in case this decision can be challenged.

Continuing to claim for your child could be worth more money overall than your child claiming UC, but it depends on all the circumstances, so get advice if you are not sure what you/your child should claim .

Universal credit amounts

Standard allowance

Single

April 2021 to September 2021:

Universal Credit amounts	April 2021/2022
Single under 25	£344*
Single 25 or over	£411.51*

*Rates have been temporarily increased by the Universal Credit (Extension of Coronavirus Measures) Regulations 2021/313

October 2021 to March 2022:

Universal Credit amounts	**October 21 to March 22**
Single under 25	£257.33
Single 25 or over	£324.84

Couple

April 2021 to September 2021:

Universal Credit amounts	**April to September 21**
Joint claimants both under 25	£490.60*
Joint claimants both over 25	£596.58

*Rates have been temporarily increased by the Universal Credit (Extension of Coronavirus Measures) Regulations 2021/313

October 2021 to March 2022:

Universal Credit Amounts	Rates October 21 to March 22
Joint claimants both under 25	£403.93
Joint claimants both over 25	£509.91

Child amounts	**Rates 2021-2022**
First child (born prior to 6th April 2017	£282.50
First child (born on or after April 2017 or second child and subsequent child (where an exception or transitional provision applies)	£237.08
Disabled child addition	**Rates 2021-2022**
Lower rate addition	£128.99
Higher rate addition	£402.41

For more detailed information concerning Universal credit, plus all other welfare benefits go to: https://www.gov.uk/government/publications/benefit-and-pension-rates-2021-to-2022/benefit-and-pension-rates-2021-to-2022

Child tax Credit

Child Tax Credit Is a benefit for people on low incomes responsible for children. You can normally only get this if you have an existing tax credit claim. You may get more Child Tax Credit if your child gets DLA or PIP, because there is an extra element of Child tax Credit included in the calculation. Make sure you tell the Tax Credit Office what rate of DLA or PIP your child is getting. If you are making a new claim for Child Tax Credit you will be told to claim Universal Credit instead. You can still get Child Tax Credit added to your claim if you already get Working Tax Credit (this isn't a new claim).

If your child is over 16, they will have to meet additional conditions for you to carry on getting Child Tax Credit, to do with being in full-time education. The rules are the same as for children who are not disabled; if your child leaves full-time education, you may no longer be entitled to Child Tax Credit for them.

You can't get Child Tax Credit for a young person who claims UC. If you are not sure whether a young person should

Child Tax Credit rates 2021/2022

Element	Yearly amount
The basic amount (this is known as 'the family element')	Up to £545
For each child (this is known as 'the child element')	Up to £2845
For each disabled child	Up to £3435 (on top of the child element)
For each severely disabled child	Up to £1390 (on top of the child element and the disabled child element)

Working tax credit

WTC is a benefit for people working a certain amount of hours and on a low income. It is usually only available if you already have a tax credit claim. You may also qualify for help with childcare costs within Working Tax Credit (see Childcare element of Working Tax Credit). If you are making a new claim for tax credits you will be told to claim Universal Credit (UC) instead. However, you can get Working Tax Credit if you already get Child Tax Credit (or vice versa).

Hours you work

You must work a certain number of hours a week to qualify.

Circumstance	Hours a week
Age 29 to 59	At least 30 hrs
Aged 60 or over	At least 16 hours

Disabled	At least 16 hours
Single with one or more children	At least 16 hours
Couple with one or more children	Usually at least 24 hours between you (with one of you working at least 16 hours)

Exceptions for couples with at least one child

You can claim if you work less than 24 hours a week between you and one of the following applies:

- you work at least 16 hours a week and you're disabled or aged 60 or above
- you work at least 16 hours a week and your partner is incapacitated (getting certain benefits because of disability or ill health), is entitled to Carer's Allowance, or is in hospital or prison

What counts as work

Your work can be:

- for someone else, as a worker or employee
- as someone who's self-employed
- a mixture of the two

If you're self-employed

Some self-employed people are not eligible for Working Tax Credit. To qualify, your self-employed work must aim to make a profit. It must also be commercial, regular and organised. This means you may not qualify if you do not:

- make a profit or have clear plans to make one

- work regularly
- keep business records, such as receipts and invoices
- follow any regulations that apply to your work, for example having the right licence or insurance

If the average hourly profit from your self-employed work is less than the National Minimum Wage, HM Revenue and Customs may ask you to provide:

- business records
- your business plan - find out how to write a business plan
- details of the day-to-day running of your business
- evidence that you've promoted your business - such as advertisements or flyers

Your pay

The work must last at least 4 weeks (or you must expect it to last 4 weeks) and must be paid. This can include payment in kind (for example farm produce for a farm labourer) or where you expect to be paid for the work.

Exceptions

Paid work does not include money paid:

- for a 'Rent a Room' scheme (less than £7,500 or £3,750 for joint owners)
- for work done while in prison
- as a grant for training or studying
- as a sports award

Your income

There's no set limit for income because it depends on your circumstances (and those of your partner). For example, £18,000 for a couple without children or £13,100 for a single person without children - but it can be higher if you have children, pay for approved childcare or one of you is disabled.

What you will get

You get a basic amount and extra (known as 'elements') on top of this. How much you get depends on things like your circumstances and income. The basic amount is up to £2,005 a year.

Element	Amount
You are a couple applying together	Up to £2060 a year
You are a single parent	Up to £2060 a year
You work at least 30 hours a week	Up to £830 a year
You have a disability	Up to £3240 a year

Direct payments

If your disabled child, having been assessed by your local authority, is entitled to services, you can choose to have direct payments (DP) and buy the services yourself. DP are for the stipulated services and are not affected by what you earn

Disabled facilities grant

A Disabled Facilities Grant helps to cover the cost of making essential improvements to your home. That means many people with disabilities can continue to live in their own homes. But a DFG is usually based on the recommendation of an occupational therapist.

There must be a person with a disability living in the property. If so, owner occupiers, private tenants, or landlords may get a DFG. The financial assistance can help pay for necessary adaptations to the building.

What Does a Disabled Facilities Grant Cover?

You may get the grant if the changes that you need are necessary to meet your daily needs. The list of alterations and adaptations include:

- Structural work to widen door openings and install ramps.
- Construction work to improve room and facility access (e.g. a downstairs bathroom or stairlift).
- Appliance installation to provide a heating system suitable for your needs.
- Adaptations to heating or lighting controls to make them easier to use by a disabled person.
- ***Note****: A Disabled Facilities Grant does not affect your rights to benefits and allowances.*

Disabled Facilities Grant Amount

- How much you get depends on two main factors:
- The amount of your household income.
- Whether your household savings are over £6,000.
- In some cases you may need to pay an amount towards the cost of the work to your property.

- Disabled Facilities Grant England: Up to £30,000
- Disabled Facilities Grant Wales: Up to £36,000
- Disabled Facilities Grant Northern Ireland: Up to £25,000
- Disabled Facilities Grant Scotland: Not available (you may get support for equipment and adaptations)

Disabled grants are also available to children under 18. A child with a disability can qualify without the inclusion of their parents' income. Your local council can offer you further information.

Disability Facilities Grant Payments

You will get the money either:

- In several instalments: as the work progresses.
- In one full payment: when the work gets completed.
- In most cases your council will pay the contractor directly. Another method is payment by a cheque for you to pass on to the workers. Your local council will agree the terms with you when they approve your application.
- When Do the Council Pay?
- In most cases it will be either:
- When the council is completely satisfied with the finished work.
- When you provide the council with the contractor's invoice, demand or receipt for payment.
- Disabled Facilities Grant Eligibility Criteria
- There is an eligibility criteria to qualify for Disabled Facilities Grants. A landlord can also apply for a disability

grant if they have a disabled tenant. Either you or a person living in your property must have a disability.

- You or the person that you are applying for must:
- Either own the property or live there as a tenant.
- Plan to live in the property during the full term of the grant period (currently 5 years).
- The council will need to be fully satisfied that the disability grant work is:
- Appropriate and necessary to meet the needs of the disabled person.
- Reasonable and workable depending on the age and structural condition of the property.

DFG Planning and Building Regulations Approval

You must apply for any separate or relevant planning permission and building regulations approval. The council can request you use a qualified architect or surveyor to design and oversee the work. But, you can use some of the grant to pay their fees if you get accepted.

How to Apply for a Disabled Facilities Grant

Apply for the grant through your local council housing department. As a general rule, the council will send an occupational therapist (OT) to meet you. The OT will review your circumstances and help to determine what changes you may need.

Council Authority Appeals

You can appeal to your Council Authority if are not satisfied with their decision. If you are still unhappy after an appeal you can complain to the Local Government Ombudsman.

Housing benefit

Housing benefit and council tax reduction, (help with the council tax from your local authority) depend on your income. In Northern Ireland, you may be entitled to help with the rates (see below).

These benefits depend on how many dependent children you have and the calculation will be different if your children are on DLA or PIP, so make sure the local authority know about this. In addition, the number of bedrooms allowed for in the Housing Benefit (HB) calculation could be higher if your children are unable to share a room because of disability and they are on DLA or PIP. Again make sure the local authority are aware.

If you make a new claim for Housing Benefit, you will usually be told to claim Universal Credit instead. It can include a housing element to help with the rent, and the same rules about the number of bedrooms apply. You can only make new claims for Housing Benefit in very limited circumstances, such as, if you are in temporary or certain types of supported accommodation. If you are on Housing Benefit and you move to new rented accommodation within the same local authority, you should be able to stay on Housing Benefit as long as there is no gap in your claim.

If you move into work, you may, depending on your income, still be entitled to such help but you need to inform your local authority for the benefits to be recalculated. You can use the calculator at the website www.turn2us.org.uk to check your entitlement.

Help with Council Tax & rates

Families with disabled children might be eligible for help paying your Council Tax bill, or help with rates in Northern Ireland.

Council Tax discount

Council Tax bills are always based on the assumption that there are at least two adults in your household. If there is only one adult in a property, 25 per cent is deducted from the bill. This is often known as the single person's discount. However, when counting how many people live in a property, some people can be ignored. A local authority will sometimes describe these people as being 'invisible' for Council Tax purposes.

Being discounted as a child or disabled person

The list of people classed as 'invisible' includes children under 18 years of age, full-time students, most apprentices and trainees aged under 25 and anyone who has a 'severe mental impairment', for example learning difficulties or an autistic spectrum disorder that severely affects intelligence and social functioning.

That disabled person must also get a disability benefit like Disability Living Allowance (DLA) or Personal Independence Payment (PIP) and provide a certificate from their GP confirming that they have a severe mental impairment.

Being discounted as a carer

Some carers can also be treated as invisible for Council Tax purposes. This includes a carer who is providing at least 35 hours of care a week to someone who is not their partner or a dependent child of theirs who is aged under 18.

In addition the disabled person must get:

- Attendance Allowance at either rate (only the high rate in Scotland).
- Disability Living Allowance care component at the middle or high rate (only the high rate in Scotland).
- Personal Independence Payment daily living component at either rate (only the enhanced rate in Scotland).
- The Armed Forces Independence Payment.

Council Tax Disability Reduction Scheme

The size of your Council Tax bill depends on the Council Tax 'band' that your property falls into. The higher the Council Tax band, the higher your bill will be. However, you may qualify for a reduction in the banding of your Council Tax bill if someone in your household is 'substantially and permanently disabled'.

A Council Tax disability reduction is not means-tested, so it makes no difference what income or savings you have. To get a disability reduction there must be a disabled person (this can be a child) living in your property and one of the following must also apply:

- They use a wheelchair indoors – there is no need for your property to have been specially constructed or adapted for wheelchair use, only that someone needs to use a wheelchair indoors and your property has sufficient space.
- There is a second bathroom or kitchen in your property that is needed by the disabled person – you can still qualify even if your property was not specifically adapted, as your property may always have had a second bathroom/kitchen. However, you will need to show that your child's health problems mean that this second bathroom or kitchen is needed
- Your child's disability is such that one of the rooms in your property (other than a bathroom, kitchen or toilet, and in addition to their own bedroom) is needed by and predominantly used by them. For example, this might apply where a room has been adapted specifically for your disabled child's use or where a room is used as a treatment room or to store specialist equipment. When deciding if a room is 'needed' by your child, the local authority must decide whether your child's disability is such that the use of the room in question is 'essential' or 'of major importance to his or her well-being'.

If you qualify, your property is treated as if it were in the next Council Tax band below. For example, if your property is valued under band D, you will be billed as if it were in band C. If your property already falls within the lowest band – band A – your bill will be reduced by 1/6th. Once awarded you must re-apply for a disability reduction for each new financial year.

Applying for a disability reduction

To apply for a disability reduction, contact the Council Tax department at your local council. You can ask for a reduction to be backdated to the date the qualifying conditions were first met. However, seek further advice if you live in England or Wales and are looking for more than six years' backdating.

Help with rates in Northern Ireland

Council Tax only applies to England, Scotland and Wales. In Northern Ireland people pay rates instead. If you are on a low income, you may be able to get help with paying your rates through the Rate Relief Scheme or through a rate rebate.

The Family Fund

The family Fund gives discretionary grants to families with severely disabled children under 18. They have their own definition of 'severely disabled'. The grants are for things not supplied by statutory authorities. Usually the grants are made to families on benefits, but the fund may also be able to help other families on low incomes.

Health costs

You can qualify for help with health costs, for example prescriptions and sight tests, if you receive some benefits such as Income Support, Income-based Jobseeker's Allowance, Income-related Employment and Support Allowance, or the Guarantee credit of Pension Credit . Some people on Universal Credit or tax credits may be entitled, and you may also be able to apply for help if you are on a low income. Prescriptions are free in England for under 16s, and under 19s in full-time education (as well as for some other groups, such as pregnant women), and they are also free in Wales, Scotland and Northern Ireland to everyone.

The benefit cap

The benefit cap – or household benefit cap – limits the total amount of benefits that an out-of-work family can receive. Some families are exempt from the benefit cap, and this includes anyone who has a dependent child getting Disability Living Allowance (DLA) or Personal Independence Payment (PIP). At the moment the cap is:

In London:

- £442.31 a week if you are a couple or a lone parent.
- £296.35 a week if you are a single person.

Outside London:

- £384.62 a week if you are a couple or lone parent.
- £257.69 if you are a single person.

Unless you are exempt from the benefit cap, your combined income from certain benefits is capped at a set amount. If you get more than this amount then the extra you receive is deducted from either your housing benefit or any Universal Credit payments you get.

You are exempt from the cap if you have a dependent child who gets either DLA or PIP. If you have a disabled child but have not claimed DLA or PIP for them yet, get advice about making a claim. It does not matter what rate of DLA or PIP your child gets; any award at all will mean that the benefit cap does not apply to you.

You are only exempt if you have a 'dependent' child on DLA or PIP. If a disabled child aged 16 or above either leaves education, turns 20 or claims certain benefits such as Employment and Support Allowance or Universal Credit, they stop being treated as a dependent. This means that their parent may then lose their exemption from the benefit cap.

However, anyone who is getting Carer's Allowance is exempt from the cap. This will help protect some parents whose disabled child stops being treated as a dependent. So long as that parent gets Carer's Allowance, they should remain exempt from the cap. You will also be exempt as a carer if you have an underlying entitlement to Carer's Allowance – that is, you have claimed Carer's Allowance and qualify for it but your payments are blocked by another benefit you receive.

In addition, those who get Universal Credit with a carer element are also exempt.

Is anyone else exempt?

You are exempt from the cap if you or your partner is working sufficient hours to be eligible for working tax credit. This is either 16 or 24 hours a week depending on your circumstances. If you work and get Universal Credit, you are exempt if your earnings are at least £604 in that monthly assessment period. Other groups are also exempt, such as families where a parent gets certain disability benefits.

Special rules have been introduced in Northern Ireland that mean housing benefit claimants get additional 'welfare supplementary payments' to make up any shortfall in their housing benefit because of the benefit cap.

If you lose your job or have to give up work

If you were working for at least 50 out of the 52 weeks immediately before you started claiming benefits and you either lose your job or give up work through illness, you are allowed a nine month 'grace period' before the cap is applied to your benefit income. You must not have been entitled to Employment and Support Allowance, Jobseeker's Allowance or Income Support during the time you were working.

If you get Universal Credit, and your earnings (including any partner's earnings) drop to below £604, a nine month grace period applies so long as you were earning above that amount in each of the preceding 12 months.

If you stopped work before you claimed Universal Credit, a nine month 'grace period' applies so long as your earnings had been above £604 per month in each of the preceding 12 months.

If you are affected by the benefit cap?

Get advice to see if you should be exempt from the benefit cap or could become exempt by changing your situation. For instance, if you have a disabled child but have not yet claimed DLA for them, getting a DLA award will result in you becoming exempt from the cap altogether.

If you cannot become exempt and are a housing benefit claimant, get advice about applying to your local authority for discretionary housing payments.

Benefits in Scotland

Most of the benefits that families in Scotland can claim are UK-wide and claimed from either the Department for Works and Pensions or HMRC. However, some benefits are different in Scotland, and these are run by a new agency called Social Security Scotland.

Over the next few years, Social Security Scotland will take on responsibility for an increasing number of new Scottish benefits. This includes Child Disability Payment, which will start to replace new claims for Disability Living Allowance in Scotland during 2021. Another new benefit, Adult Disability

Payment, will replace Personal Independence Payment, while a new Carer's Assistance will replace Carer's Allowance in Scotland.

The introduction of these new Scottish disability and carers benefits was delayed by the coronavirus outbreak. During 2021, new claims for Disability Living Allowance will be replaced by Child Disability Payment, a new benefit administered by Social Security Scotland.

For more advice concerning benefit entitlement in Scotland go to:
https://contact.org.uk/help-for-families/information-advice-services/benefits-financial-help/benefits-and-tax-credits/welfare-benefits-in-scotland.

****

Useful contacts

Attendance Allowance helpline 0800 731 0122 Textphone 0800 731 0317

Carer's Allowance Unit 0800 731 0297 (textphone: 0800 731 0317)

DWP Bereavement Service:
Telephone: 0800 731 0469
Textphone: 0800 731 0464

Department for Work and pensions
www.gov.uk/government/organisations/department-for-work-pensions

Winter Fuel Payments Helpline 0800 731 0160

Disability benefits Advice
www.gov.uk/disability-benefits-helpline
0800 121 4433
Textphone 0800 121 4493
Jobcentre Plus 0800 055 6688

Pension Credit claim line 0800 99 1234 (textphone: 0800 169 0133).

Royal National Institute for the Blind 0303 123 9999 www.rnib.org.uk.

Tax Credit helpline 0345 300 3900 (textphone 0345 300 3909).

TV Licence concessions 0300 790 6165

Universal Credit helpline 0800 328 5644 Textphone 0800 328 1344

Child benefit helpline 0300 200 3100: textphone 0300 200 3103

Family Fund www.familyfund.org.uk

Healthy Start Helpline 0345 607 6823 www.healthystart.nhs.uk

www.nurserymilk.co.uk.

*****

Chapter 5

Disabled People and Education

It goes without saying that the last 15 months of the pandemic, and the associated lockdowns, have greatly disrupted education for all, as well as disabled children. Thankfully at the time of writing the situation is slowly getting back to normal.

Education and the law

It's against the law for a school or other education provider to treat disabled students unfavourably. This includes: 'direct discrimination', eg refusing admission to a student because of disability; 'indirect discrimination', eg only providing application forms in one format that may not be accessible; 'discrimination arising from a disability', eg a disabled pupil is prevented from going outside at break time because it takes too long to get there; 'harassment', eg a teacher shouts at a disabled student for not paying attention when the student's disability stops them from easily concentrating and victimisation, eg suspending a disabled student because they've complained about harassment.

Reasonable adjustments

As with employers, an education provider has a duty to make 'reasonable adjustments' to make sure disabled students are not discriminated against. These changes could include changes to physical features, eg creating a ramp so that students can enter a classroom,providing extra support and aids (like specialist teachers or equipment)

Portage

It is worth at this point mentioning portage, which can benefit your child pre-school. Portage is a home-visiting educational service for pre-school children with additional support needs and their families. Portage Home Visitors are employed by Local Authorities and Charities to support children and families within their local community.

The Portage model of learning is characterised by the following attributes:

- regular home visiting;
- supporting the development of play, communication, relationships, and learning for young children within the family;
- supporting the child and family's participation and inclusion in the community in their own right;
- working together with parents within the family, with them taking the leading role in the partnership that is established;

- helping parents to identify what is important to them and their child and plan goals for learning and participation;
- keeping a shared record of the child's progress and other issues raised by the family;
- responding flexibly to the needs of the child and family when providing support;
- You can find out more about Portage by contacting The National Portage Association, address at the end of the chapter.

Special Educational Needs (SEN)

All publicly-funded pre-schools, nurseries, state schools and local authorities must try to identify and help assess children with Special Educational Needs. If a child has a statement of special educational needs, they should have a 'transition plan' drawn up in Year 9. This helps to plan what support the child will have after leaving school.

Higher education

All universities and higher education colleges should have a person in charge of disability issues that you can talk to about the support they offer. You can also ask local social services for an assessment to help with your day-to-day living needs.

Special educational needs support

Your child will get SEN support at their school or college. Your child may need an education, health and care (EHC) plan if they need more support than their school provides.

Children under 5

SEN support for children under 5 includes:

- a written progress check when your child is 2 years old
- a child health visitor carrying out a health check for your child if they're aged 2 to 3
- a written assessment in the summer term of your child's first year of primary school
- making reasonable adjustments for disabled children, like providing aids like tactile signs

Nurseries, playgroups and childminders registered with Ofsted follow the Early Years Foundation Stage (EYFS) framework. The framework makes sure that there's support in place for children with SEND.

Talk to a doctor or health adviser if you think your child has SEND but they don't go to a nursery, playgroup or childminder. They'll tell you what support options are available.

Children between 5 and 15

Talk to the teacher or the SEN co-ordinator (SENCO) if you think your child needs:

- a special learning programme
- extra help from a teacher or assistant

- to work in a smaller group
- observation in class or at break
- help taking part in class activities
- extra encouragement in their learning, eg to ask questions or to try something they find difficult
- help communicating with other children
- support with physical or personal care difficulties, eg eating, getting around school safely or using the toilet

Young people aged 16 or over in further education

Contact the college before your child starts further education to make sure that they can meet your child's needs. The college and your local authority will talk to your child about the support they need.

Extra help

An education, health and care (EHC) plan is for children and young people aged up to 25 who need more support than is available through special educational needs support. EHC plans identify educational, health and social needs and set out the additional support to meet those needs.

Requesting an EHC assessment

You can ask your local authority to carry out an assessment if you think your child needs an EHC plan. A young person can request an assessment themselves if they're aged 16 to 25.

A request can also be made by anyone else who thinks an assessment may be necessary, including doctors, health visitors, teachers, parents and family friends. If they decide to carry out an assessment you may be asked for:

- any reports from your child's school, nursery or childminder
- doctors' assessments of your child
- a letter from you about your child's needs

The local authority will tell you within 16 weeks whether an EHC plan is going to be made for your child.

Creating an EHC plan

Your local authority will create a draft EHC plan and send you a copy. You have 15 days to comment, including if you want to ask that your child goes to a specialist needs school or specialist college. Your local authority has 20 weeks from the date of the assessment to give you the final EHC plan.

Disagreeing with a decision

You can challenge your local authority about:

- their decision to not carry out an assessment
- their decision to not create an EHC plan
- the special educational support in the EHC plan
- the school named in the EHC plan

If you can't resolve the problem with your local authority, you can appeal to the Special Educational Needs and Disability (SEND) Tribunal.

Personal budgets

You may be able to get a personal budget for your child if they have an EHC plan or have been told that they need one. It allows you to have a say in how to spend the money on support for your child.

There are 3 ways you can use your personal budget. You can have:

- direct payments made into your account - you buy and manage services yourself
- an arrangement with your local authority or school where they hold the money for you but you still decide how to spend it (sometimes called 'notional arrangements')
- third-party arrangements - you choose someone else to manage the money for you

You can have a combination of all 3 options.

Independent support for children of all ages

Independent supporters can help you and your child through the new SEN assessment process, including:

- replacing a statement of special educational needs with a new EHC plan
- moving a child from a learning difficulty assessment (LDA) to an EHC plan

You can find out how to get local support through:

- Council for Disabled Children
- Information, Advice and Support Service Network
- your local authority website and search for 'Local Offer'

Early Years Action and School Action

This support is either a different way of teaching certain things, or some help from an extra adult.

Early Years Action Plus and School Action Plus

This is extra help from an external specialist, eg a speech therapist.

Assessments

An assessment of special educational needs involves experts and people involved in your child's education. They ask about your child's needs and what should be done to meet them.

Statement

A statement of special education needs describes your child's needs and how they should be met, including what school they should go to.

Further education

If your child has a statement of special educational needs, they'll have a 'transition plan' drawn up in Year 9. This helps to plan for their future after leaving school.

Disabled people and financing studies

Financial support for all students comes in the form of tuition fee loans, means tested loans for living expenses and also a range of supplementary grants and loans depending on individual circumstances. Entitlement to student support depends on where you are living and where you intend to study. For details of loan entitlement and rates also Bursaries, you should contact:

Student finance England if you reside in England www.gov.uk/student-finance

Northern Ireland Student finance NI 0300 100 0077 www.studentfinanceni.co.uk

Scotland Student Awards Agency for Scotland www.saas.gov.uk

Wales Student Finance Wales 0300 200 4050 www.studentfianncewales.co.uk

For details of loans and bursaries plus other sources of finance, you should contact the student support officer responsible for advice at the educational institution that you are to attend.

Students and means tested benefits

If you are a disabled student and want more information on benefits entitlement and how being a student in higher education affects benefits then you should contact the Disability Advisor at your local Jobcentre Plus. Essentially, benefit entitlement will depend very much on your individual circumstances and what type of education you are undertaking.

****

Useful contacts

Contact a Family helpline

helpline@cafamily.org.uk

Telephone: 0808 808 3555

Independent Parental Special Education Advice (IPSEA).

24-26 Gold Street

Saffron Walden

Essex

CB10 1EJ

www.ipsea.org.uk

Telephone: 01799 582030 (Monday to Friday, 9am-5pm)

National Portage Association

Kings Court

17 School Road

Birmingham

B28 8JG Tel: 0121 244 1807

Fax: 0121 244 1801

www.portage.org.uk

General Enquiries info@portage.org.uk

****

Chapter 6

Help With Transport and Equipment for You and Your Disabled Child

---

You can obtain help and assistance with transport and equipment, which is designed specifically to make life easier for you and your child. Assistance with transport and equipment will also help to foster independence for your child.

This chapter outlines the main sources of transport and equipment available for you, but for more detailed advice about equipment for use inside and outside your home you should discuss this with your occupational therapist.

Welfare benefits

We covered general welfare benefits in chapter 4. In addition to the various welfare benefits available, there are other schemes, the most important being the schemes to help you buy a car and the Blue Badge Scheme that relates to parking for the disabled. You can also get exemption from Vehicle Road Tax.

Blue Badge parking concessions-What is the Blue Badge Scheme?

The aim of the Blue Badge scheme is to help disabled people who have severe mobility problems to access goods, services and other facilities by allowing them to park close to their destination. The scheme provides a national range of on-street parking concessions for Blue Badge holders who are travelling either as a driver or passenger. Councils can charge a fee, usually £10 for a badge.

People who automatically qualify for a badge

You're automatically eligible for a Blue Badge if you:

- are registered as blind
- get the higher rate of the mobility component of Disability Living Allowance (DLA)
- get Personal Independence Payment (PIP) and scored 8 points or more in the 'moving around' area of your assessment - check your decision letter if you're not sure
- get War Pensioners' Mobility Supplement
- received a lump sum payment as part of the Armed Forces Compensation scheme (tariffs 1 to 8), and have been certified as having a permanent and substantial disability

People who may also qualify for a badge

It's worth applying as you might still be able to get a badge. You'll have to fill in an extra part of the application to show why you need one.

You should do this if:

- you have problems walking that are permanent, or that your doctor says are likely to last at least a year
- you can't use your arms
- you're applying on behalf of a child aged over 2 who has problems walking, or a child under 3 who needs to be close to a vehicle because of a health condition

You can find out more about the Blue Badge Scheme and whether you are entitled by contacting your local council. Alternatively, you can contact the National blue badge helpline on 0800 0699 784. Also, a very good site to find out more in-depth information about the scheme is https://www.citizensadvice.org.uk/benefits/sick-or-disabled-people-and-carers/help-for-disabled-travellers1/blue-badge-scheme/applying-for-a-blue-badge. This is the website of the Citizens Advice Bureau.

The Motability Scheme

he Motability Scheme helps disabled people get mobile by exchanging their mobility allowance to lease a car, scooter or powered wheelchair. To be eligible to join the Scheme, you need to receive one of the following mobility allowances and must have at least 12 months' award length of your allowance remaining.

Higher Rate Mobility Component of Disability Living Allowance (HRMC DLA)

This allowance is provided by the Department for Work and Pensions (DWP) and can be used to cover the cost of a lease agreement with Motability Operations Ltd. As of April 2021, this allowance is £62.55 per week.

As part of its welfare reform programme, the Government has started to replace Disability Living Allowance (DLA) with a new benefit called Personal Independence Payment (PIP) for disabled people aged between 16 and 64. The Motability Scheme works with PIP in the same way as is it does with DLA. For more information, go to dwp.gov.uk/pipOpens in new window . As of April 2021, this allowance is £62.55 per week.

War Pensioners' Mobility Supplement (WPMS)

This allowance is provided by Veterans UK ttps://www.gov.uk/government/organisations/veterans-uk

and can be used to cover the cost of a lease agreement with Motability Operations Ltd. As of April 2021, this allowance is £69.85 per week.

Veterans gateway is also a very useful organisation which provides help and support:

https://www.veteransgateway.org.uk

Armed Forces Independence Payment (AFIP)

Those who receive this allowance will be eligible to join the Motability Scheme. For more information, visit Veterans UK. As of April 2021, this allowance is £62.55 per week (this refers to the mobility element, which is the same rate as HRMC DLA and ERMC PIP).

If you are visiting the Car Search or Scooter and Powered Wheelchair Search to compare and choose a Motability vehicle, please refer to the DLA/PIP option when making your allowance choice on the relevant option.

The Attendance Allowance cannot be used to lease a car through the Motability Scheme

You may not have to pay VAT on having a vehicle adapted to suit your condition, or on the lease of a Motability vehicle - this is known as VAT relief.

There are currently over 640,000 people enjoying the benefits of Motability. The following are included in the package:

- A brand new car, powered wheelchair or scooter every three years, or Wheelchair Accessible Vehicle (WAV) every five years
- Insurance, servicing and maintenance
- Full breakdown assistance
- Annual vehicle tax
- Replacement tyres (and batteries for scooters and wheelchairs)
- Windscreen repair or replacement
- 60,000 mileage allowance over three years for cars; 100,000 for WAVs
- Many adaptations at no extra cost
- Two named drivers for your car

The Motability Scheme is directed and overseen by Motability, a national charity that also raises funds and provides financial assistance to customers who would otherwise be unable to afford the mobility solution they need.

Motability Operations is a company responsible for the finance, administration and maintenance of Motability cars, scooters and powered wheelchairs.

To find out more about Motability you should contact them at the address at the end of this chapter.

Use of Public Transport-Travel permits for buses and trains

Most local authorities offer travel permits for children who are disabled and over the age of 5 years. There is normally a charge, as there is with everything and the criteria and availability of the permits will vary according to each authority, generally however, the main criteria is being in receipt of the higher rate of PIP. In some cases, your child's GP may be asked for a supporting letter. Your local council will be able to help in this regard.

Help with taxi fares

Some local councils, but not all, offer help with the cost of Black Cab taxi fares. The criteria is similar to other concessions. You should ask at your local council for details.

Community transport schemes

Many local authorities offer local community transport schemes for people with mobility problems. Again, the local authority will have details of schemes on offer in your area. There is also a national association, the Community Transport Association. The CTA is a national membership association which leads and supports community transport. Address at the end of this chapter.

Equipment available for disabled children-Equipment provision through local authorities & direct payments

Much of the equipment need by you or your child, may be provided by your local authority. This will usually occur following an assessment and recommendation by an occupational therapist and will depend on the eligibility criteria of your local authority. If your child is eligible, the equipment will be provided on a long-term loan basis. This means that the equipment will remain the property of the council, but that your child can use it for as long as they need it. The council will take responsibility for the servicing and maintenance of the equipment.

Direct payments

If your child's occupational therapy assessment shows that they need a piece of equipment but you prefer an alternative piece of equipment that meets the same need, you may be able to have a direct payment. It is now mandatory for local authorities to offer the choice of direct payments.

A direct payment is a cash payment that equals the amount it costs your local authority to supply their choice of standard equipment. You can then add your own money to this ('top-up') to buy your preferred piece of equipment. For example, your local authority may provide you with a bath lift that has a fixed angle backrest and you may wish to pay for a bath lift that has a reclining backrest. Usually you will be the joint owner of the equipment with your local authority.

Before you purchase the equipment, your local authority must be satisfied that your child's needs will be met by the item you have chosen, and that the equipment is safe. You will also need to agree with your local authority who will be responsible for the servicing and maintenance of the equipment. Following purchase, you will need to provide proof of purchase and your local authority will review the equipment to ensure safety and suitability. Note that if you receive direct payments to arrange your child's care and support at home then this must not be used to buy equipment.

Arranging an assessment

To enquire about an assessment with an occupational therapist contact your local social services. You can obtain their contact details by entering your postcode on the directgov website.

Wheelchairs

If you have a long-term or permanent difficulty with mobility, getting a wheelchair or scooter, or other mobility equipment, may help you to live more independently.

Again, you will need to consult an occupational therapist who will provide you with the advice appropriate to your specific situation. there are wheelchairs centres in each local authority area and in Scotland and Wales they are called Aritificial limb and appliance centres and in Northern Ireland they are called Prosthetic and Orthotic Aids Centres.

Other needs such as nappies and incontinence pads

If you require nappies or incontince pads, and your child is over the age of infancy, as a result of an ongoing disability, you should contact your local health authority. Your GP can advise you about what is avialble or at least point you in the right direction, as can the Health Visitor or Community Paediatrician.

****

Useful Contacts

Motability

www.motability.co.uk

Tel: 0300 456 4566 8am-7pm Monday to Friday 9am-1pm Saturday.

Blue badge Scheme

www.gov.uk/blue-badge-scheme-information-council

National blue badge helpline 0800 0699 784.

Community Transport Association

0161 351 1475

www.ctauk.org

Shelter England

www.shelter.org.uk

Disability Housing Scotland

www.housingoptionsscotland.org.uk

Independent Living For Disabled people

www.scope.org.uk

0808 800 3333

www.gov.uk/help-for-disabled-child

Deals with UK housing advice for disabled

Chapter 7

Holidays and Breaks for Disabled Children and Their Families

Holidays and breaks for everyone have been disrupted by COVID 19, this includes disabled children, who have had to be shielded during the pandemic.. Hopefully, at the time of writing this situation is easing and the information below will help parents of disabled children to find out what holidays and breaks are available both for them and for the children.

Everyone, whatever their situation, needs a break from their children every now and again. Having a breathing space from caring for a disabled child is no exception. Also, your disabled child is likely to enjoy the opportunity of doing new things with other children and adults and will also probably learn much from the experience.

In addition to breaks away from your child(ren) breaks away with your child are also important and there are many organisations which can help you plan a holiday with your disabled child.

In this chapter we outline some of the possibilities for short-term breaks or respite care, such as family based schemes, play schemes or residential care, and holidays. There is also a list of organisations which may be of use to you.

Respite breaks or short term breaks

Respite care is often used to describe the situation when a child goes away from the family home overnight to give his or her parent/carer a break. In addition, respite care can also apply to care given to a child in his or her own home whilst the parent/carer goes out, and to short-term breaks during the day, such as play schemes.

Many parents find it very hard to be away from their child, even when they really need the break. This is understandable but can be overcome by planning respite care so that you and your child can get to know someone over a space of time before you leave them in charge of your child. Because respite care may be needed in an emergency - if you were taken ill, for example, and there was no one else to care for your child - is it important for you to check out the respite care possibilities at an early stage before any crisis may occur.

Different types of respite care and short-term breaks are listed and described below.

Family Based Respite Care

Family based respite care schemes are usually run by local voluntary agencies or by social services departments. They assess, recruit, train and monitor single people or families who are able to look after a disabled child in their home on a regular basis, like 1 night a fortnight, a weekend per month, or sometimes longer spells like a week or a fortnight on occasions (e.g. once/twice a year) so the parent(s) can go away.

The procedure for recruiting, assessing and approving carers is very thorough and governed by Children Act 1989 guidelines (as amended by ongoing regulations) and is very similar to the procedure for recruiting foster parents. So you can rest assured from the start that the carer matched to your child is as suitable and capable as possible.

The scheme which recruits carers for a disabled child will have information about you and your child, what the child is like, what his or her disabilities are and what his or her likes and dislikes are. They will then match you and your child with a carer they judge to be suitable for your child. They will try and match racial, cultural and religious backgrounds as far as possible. It is then usual for you and your child to meet with the prospective carer and his or her own family on several occasions, at your home and the carer's home, to get to know each other. Only after a few meetings will it be possible for your child to stay overnight at the carer's home.

Family based respite care does not always have to mean overnight care though. Many carers are willing and able to take care of children during the day during the week on occasions (during the school holidays occasionally, for example) or sometimes at the weekend. This can normally be negotiated with the carer and who ever is running the scheme.

Residential Respite Care

Residential respite care units for disabled children are run by health, social services or voluntary agencies. They offer overnight care for your child on an emergency or regular basis, if you meet certain criteria which varies depending on the unit. If you are able to plan your child's first stay, it is always best to visit the unit with your child to meet the staff and look around the facilities. This will mean that parting from your child and seeing your child go away from home will be much easier for you both. You can find out about what residential respite care is available by asking your health professional, social services department or voluntary agency.

Play schemes and After School Clubs

Plays schemes for the school holidays and after school clubs are normally run by the leisure department of your local council, although some are also run by voluntary agencies. They are normally based in schools and offer play activities and outings in a relaxed but supervised environment.

Your child may be able to join the play schemes and clubs run for non-disabled children, depending on what his or her needs are. Special schemes and clubs are also run for disabled children.

Respite Care or Short-term Breaks in Your Home

There may be opportunities for respite care in your home meaning that your child can stay at home whilst you go out. This type of respite care, however, is not normally for overnights. Such breaks will usually be for care during the day, such as 2-4 hours, to give you time to go shopping, see some friends, or simply spend some time alone or with your partner. One of the main national organisations offering this type of care is the Carers Trust, which was a merger between Crossroads Caring For Carers Scheme and the Princess Royal Trust for Carers. They employ carers who go into families once a week for 4 hours or twice a week for 2 hours. Most families receive a maximum of 4 hours per week but this depends on their needs and circumstances. Carers work all hours so it is possible to have help at weekends and evenings as well as during the day. Carers Trust carers work with children and people of all ages and all disabilities.

Some local Crossroads Caring for Carers schemes also offer an occasional night sitting service if your sleep is often interrupted. Some areas may not have a Carers Trust scheme but will have a similar scheme which works under a different name. Ask the Carers Trust national organisation (address at the end of this chapter) or your local social services department, health professional or voluntary organisation to see if you have a local scheme.

Holidays

Having a disabled child should not mean that you cannot go away. There are many organisations that can help you plan a holiday with your child or who can organise an independent trip for him or her if s/he is old enough.

The numerous organisations listed overleaf publish information about holidays for the disabled including family holidays, activity holidays and holidays for unaccompanied disabled children and adults.

Useful Contacts

Holiday Care
0843 289 2459
www.holiday-care.co.uk

Disability Rights UK
14 East Bay Lane
Here East
Queen Elizabeth Olympic Park
Stratford
London
E15 2GW

Office Number: 0330 995 0400
This line is not an advice line. There are various different advice lines on the website.
Email: enquiries@disabilityrightsuk.

Disability Holidays
Registered Office:
Unit 8 Victoria Way
Newmarket
Suffolk
CB8 7SH
Email: admin@disabilityholidaysguide.com

The following organisations can provide holidays and holiday accommodation for disabled children and their families.

Break
1 Montague Road
Schofield House,
Spar Road,
Norwich,
Norfolk NR6 6BX
email reception@break-charity.or
www.break-charity.org

Specialises in holidays for multiply disabled children and adults, individuals, groups and those unaccompanied by parents or staff

St Mark's Community Centre
218 Tollgate Road
Beckton
London
E6 5YA

Telephone: 0207 474 1687
Fax: 0207 473 7847
e-mail enquiries: contactus@across.org.uk

THE CALVERT TRUST

For all enquries relating to The Lake District Calvert Trust or general Calvert Trust questions please contact them using the details below.

Telephone: 017687 72255
Facsimile: 017687 71920
http://www.calvert-trust.org.uk/contact-us/lake-district

KESWICK
Little Crosthwaite
Keswick
Cumbria CA12 4QD
017687 72255
www.calvert-trust.keswick

EXMOOR
Wislandpound Farm
Kentisbury
North Devon EX31 4SJ
01598 763221
www.calvert-trust.org.uk/exmoor
The Calvert Trust in Northumberland, Cumbria and Devon have purpose built centres for disabled people and their families offering a wide range of sports and recreational activities.

3H Fund (Help the Handicapped Holiday Fund)
B2, Speldhurst Business Park,
Langton Road,
Speldhurst, Tunbridge Wells, Kent TN3 0AQ
Tel: 01892 860207
Email: info@3hfund.org.uk
Group holidays for physically disabled children and young people over 11 years.

FINANCING HOLIDAYS

Social Services/children's services

Disabled children and their families may be able to obtain a small grant from their social services department towards a holiday. The criteria for receiving some funding will vary from one council to another, but many means test and/or will only give money to a family every few years.

Charitable Organisations

MENCAP

https://www.mencap.org.uk/
0808 808 111
Email: holidayfund@mencap.org.uk
Provides grants towards the cost of a holiday for individuals with learning disabilities.

THE FAMILY FUND

Unit 4, Alpha Court

Monks Cross Drive

Huntington

York Y32 9WN

01904 550055

www.familyfund.org.uk

info@familyfund.org.uk

To receive funding, there must be a severely disabled child under the age of 16 in the family. Grants vary in size and can be used towards family holidays with or without the disabled child.

THE FAMILY HOLIDAY ASSOCIATION

7-14 Great Dover Street

London

SE1 4YR

020 3117 0650

www.familyholidayassociation.org.uk

The Family Holiday Association provides grants for families for one week's holiday of their choice. The family must be referred to the Association by social services, health professional or local voluntary organization. The child must be at least 3 years old.

FAMILY ACTION

Family Action Head Office
34 Wharf Road

London
N1 7GR
Telephone: 020 7254 6251
info@family-action.org.uk
https://www.family-action.org.uk

Provides grants for holidays to families with disabled children. Applications are made through social services or health professional.

Trains

Complaints and information-National Rail Enquiries Tel – 03457 48 49 50. If you aren't happy with the way a train company deals with your complaint you can appeal, outside London, to: Passenger Focus (tel: 0300 123 2170).

In London-London Travel Watch at:
http://www.londontravelwatch.org.uk/ (tel: 020 3176 2999).

Air Travel

Complaints and information- Civil Aviation Authority (CAA) at the address below:

Passenger Advice and Complaints Team
https://www.caa.co.uk/Our-work/About-us/Contact-us

Taxi and Mini cabs

Public Carriage Office (PCO)
https://pcolicencehq.co.uk/contact

Specialist companies

Responsible Travel

Access Travel

Tel: 01273 823 700

www.responsibletravel.com

Enable Holidays

www.enableholidays.com

0871 222 4939

****

Chapter 8

Disability and Employment

As with all areas of life, employment opportunities for all, and in particular disabled people, have been greatly affected by the pandemic. As with all other areas covered in this book, things are gradually getting back to normal.

Although this book is about the rights of disabled children, there might come a time, depending on the nature of your child's disability, when he or she wants to enter the workplace. This chapter covers the support and training available to help disabled people into work. It also covers employers responsibilities towards disabled people in the workplace.

Entering employment

The role of Jobcentre plus and Disability Employment Advisors

Jobcentre plus is the Department of Work and Pensions organisation providing benefits and services to people of working age. This means age 16 or over. Everyone who claims benefits from Jobcentre Plus is allocated a personal advisor to deal with claims for benefit and help them back into work. Disabled people also have access to a Disability Employment

Advisor who provide employment assessment, job seeking advice and assistance with training as well as specialist advice and information. It is important to note that advice and support from a DEA is not dependant on benefits it is available to any disabled person.

Work programmes

There are a number of work programmes managed by 'providers' who are contracted by the government which aim to help people find work and stay in work. They provide activities such as work experience, work trials, help to become self-employed, voluntary work, training and ongoing support. The programmes are mandatory if a person is considered capable of work. Referral to work programmes is normally through Jobcentre Plus. If in receipt of Job Seekers Allowance a person will have to take part in the Work Programme after nine months. If the advisor agrees a person may join earlier than this if they wish. If they receive Employment and Support Allowance the time for entry to a Work Programme will vary depending on an assessment of a person's fitness to work.

Community Work Placement Programme

The Community Work Placement Programme was designed for Jobseeker's Allowance claimants who require further support to obtain and sustain employment following a Work Programme placement. Participants had to undertake work placements for the benefit of the community and work-related activity. This programme was mandatory. It has now been withdrawn.

Access to Work www.gov.uk/access-to-work

Access to Work is designed to help disabled people overcome any barriers that they may face in obtaining employment and retaining employment. Access to Work provides practical advice and also grants towards extra costs which may be incurred arising from a disability. This advice and support can include special aids and adaptations, or equipment needed for employment, adaptations premises (not new) and equipment, help with travel, help with a support worker, a communicator and, if needed, an interpreter.

Certain types of expenditure are excluded, details of which can be obtained during the application stage. Costs which are the responsibility of the employer, for example costs which are seen as a 'reasonable adjustment' under the Equality Act 2010, are not included. (See below for details of 'reasonable adjustments').

A person will be eligible for help through the Access to Work scheme if they are employed, including as an apprentice, self-employed or unemployed and have a job to start and they are disabled. Access to Work defines disability as in the Equality Act 2010 (see introduction) but also includes impairments and health conditions that are only evident in the workplace.

Access to Work also provides help to people with mental health conditions and learning difficulties. The service provides a wide range of support for a period of six months for people with mental health conditions, including work focussed mental health support tailored to the individual, assessment of an individuals needs, a personalised support plan, advice and guidance to employers and the identification of reasonable adjustments needed in the workplace.

How much support can a person receive?

If a person has been in a job for less than six weeks, are self-employed or are about to start work, Access to Work will cover 100% of approved costs. If they have been employed for six weeks or more when they apply for help, Access to Work will pay only some of the costs of support, called 'cost sharing' which is dependant on the number of employees in an organisation. The funding agreements can last up to three years with an annual review.

You can apply for access to work online https://www.gov.uk/access-to-work/apply or by phone, 0800 121 7459. Normally there will be a telephone interview by an advisor to assess eligibility.

Training

There are numerous government training programmes designed to help prepare people for work. Details can be found from a nearest Jobcentre Plus office. There are many courses available designed to help disabled people. Contact a disabled employment advisor at the local Jobcentre Plus office or ring the National Careers Service Helpline 0800 100 900 or Skills Development Scotland 0800 917 8000.

Benefits while training

DLA and PIP are not usually affected if training is undertaken or if a person gets a training allowance. However, DLA care component and PIP daily living component will not usually be paid for any days that a person stays in a care home to attend a residential training programme. The residential training programmes aim to help long-term unemployed adults overcome disability related barriers to employment.

Advice concerning benefits entitlement, such as Universal Credit Income Support, Jobseeker's allowance and Employment and Support Allowance and how they are affected by training, can be obtained from a local Jobcentre Plus.

When a person is in work-Disability and employers responsibilities

It's against the law for employers to discriminate against anyone because of a disability. The Equality Act 2010 protects everyone and covers areas including:

- application forms
- interview arrangements
- aptitude or proficiency tests
- job offers
- terms of employment, including pay

- promotion, transfer and training opportunities
- dismissal or redundancy
- discipline and grievances

Reasonable adjustments in the workplace

Those employees with disabilities share the same employment rights as other workers with the addition of some other rights as stated within the Equality Act 2010. Within this act, employers are expected to make 'reasonable adjustments' within the workplace with regard to access and facilities for disabled members of staff. The provisions set out in the Equality Act apply to every employer, no matter the size or industry (except the armed forces). It is worth noting that the reasonable adjustment requirements are not necessary to carry out in anticipation or only in case an employer gains a disabled employee. The adjustments need only be carried out once a disabled person is employed or applies for a role within the company.

To comply with the Equality Act 2010, an employee must suffer from severe or long-term impairments. Impairments of disabled employees include:

- Physical impairments - mobility disabilities
- Mental impairments - long term (12 months plus) mental illnesses or learning disabilities
- Sensory impairments - visual or hearing impairments.

What are reasonable adjustments?

The Equality Act states employers have a duty to amend the workplace in order to accommodate both disabled employees and/or applicants for job roles. These adjustments are in order to avoid disabled people being at a disadvantage when applying for a job or indeed working within an organisation. Reasonable adjustments can vary and cover areas from working arrangements to physical changes around the workplace.

Adjusted working arrangements may be flexible working hours to allow disabled employees to be able to meet their employment requirements, or amendments being made to workplace equipment, adapting it to suit employee's capabilities.

If a physical feature within the workplace creates a disadvantage for a disabled employee, steps must be taken to amend or remove the obstruction. Physical adjustments can include changes such as:

- The addition of a ramp rather than steps to access buildings.
- Providing disabled toilet facilities need to provided to accommodate those that need them.
- The widening of doorways to allow for wheelchair access.
- Repositioning door handles and/or light switches etc to ensure they can be reached.

In some cases, an employer may need to provide disabled employees with extra help through an aid to ensure that the disabled employee is not at any disadvantage against other workers. This aid may be in form of specialist or adapted equipment, such as special computer keyboards or telephones.

With regard to a disabled person applying for a job, an employer does not necessarily need to make the physical adjustments before the interview. It will suffice that an easily accessible location and necessary support and assistance for the applicant to get there is provided. If the applicant is then employed, the employer must consider the other adjustments mentioned above.

Recruitment

An employer who is recruiting staff may make limited enquiries about a person's health or disability. They can only be asked about their health or disability:

- to help decide if they can carry out a task that is an essential part of the work
- to help find out if they can take part in an interviewto help decide if the interviewers need to make reasonable adjustments for them in a selection process
- to help monitoring
- if they want to increase the number of disabled people they employ
- if they need to know for the purposes of national security checks

A person may be asked whether they have a health condition or disability on an application form or in an interview. Thought needs to be given as to whether the question is one that is allowed to be asked at that stage of recruitment.

Redundancy and retirement

A person can't be chosen for redundancy just because they are disabled. The selection process for redundancy must be fair and balanced for all employees. Also, an employer cannot force a person to retire if they become disabled.

****

Useful Contacts

Access to Work.0800 121 7459
https://www.gov.uk/access-to-work

www.evenbreak.co.uk
Jobs for disabled people - Evenbreak matches disabled job seekers with employers looking to build a diverse workforce

Evenbreak
402 Metro Central Heights
London SE1 6DX
www.evenbreak.co.uk
Email Address:
info@evenbreak.co.uk
0845 658 5717

www.gov.uk/rights-disabled-person/employment

Industrial Injuries
John Rideal House
29 Shambles Street,
Barnsley
S70 2SA
0845 603 1358
https://www.gov.uk/industrial-injuries-disablement-benefit

National Careers Service Helpline 0800 100 900 or Skills Development Scotland 0800 917 8000.

*****

Index

Activity holidays, 127

Access to work, 137

Adaptations, 85

Adoptions, 61, 65

Agency Workers, 66

Air travel, 133

Ante-natal classes. 64

Anxiety, 26

Armed forces independence payment, 116

Asthma, 26

Attention deficit hyperactivity disorder, 10

Autistic spectrum disorders, 26

Bi-polar disorder, 26

Blue Badge parking, 114

Blue badge Scheme, 114

Calvert Trust, 130

Cancer, 26

Cardiovascular disease, 26

Carers Allowance, 73

Cerebra, 45

Challenging Behavior Foundation, 13

Child benefit, 70

Child tax credit, 80

Childline, 10

Chronic fatigue syndrome, 26

Clinical psychologist, 39

Communication support worker, 42
Community transport schemes, 118
Contact a family, 46
Coronavirus, 9, 10, 12
Council for disabled people, 12
Council Tax Support, 89
COVID 19, 9, 123
Crossroads, 127
CrySis, 22

Dementia, 26
Department for Education, 47
Depression, 18, 26
Dietician, 40
Disability Employment Advisors, 135
Disability Living Allowance, 68
Disabled children, 34
Disabled Facilities Grant, 84
Disability Rights UK, 37, 47
Dyslexia, 26
Dyspraxia, 26

Early Years Action, 108
Eating disorders, 26
Education, 101
Education Health and Care Plan, 105
Educational psychologist, 40
Employment law, 135
Epilepsy, 26
Equality Act 2010, 23

Equipment, 113

Family and Childcare Trust, 47
Family Based Respite Care, 124
Family Lives, 22
Fibromyalgia, 26

General practitioner (GP), 40

Health visitor, 40
Heart disease, 26
Higher education, 103
HIV, 26
Holidays, 127
Housing Benefit, 88

Impairment, 25

Key worker, 41
KIDS, 21

Learning disabilities, 26
Learning disability nurses, 41
LIMB POWER, 13
Low mood, 26

Maternity leave, 53
MENCAP, 22
Motability, 115

Motability Scheme, 115
Motor neurone disease, 26
Multiple sclerosis, 26
Muscular dystrophy, 26
Myalgic encephalitis, 26

Named officer, 42
National Portage Association, 111
NSPCC, 17

Obsessive compulsive disorder, 26

Paediatric neurologist, 43
Paediatric occupational therapist, 42
Paediatrician (Health Service), 42
Pandemic, 9
Parental leave, 59
Pension Credit, 76
Personal Independence Payment, 68
Personality disorder, 26
Physiotherapist, 43
Play schemes, 126
Portage, 43, 102
Portage home visitor, 43
Post traumatic stress disorder, 26
Professionals, 38
Public transport, 113

Reasonable adjustments, 102, 140

Recruitment, 142
Redundancy, 143
Residential Respite Care, 125
Respiratory conditions, 26
Respite breaks, 124
Rheumatoid arthritis, 26

Schizophrenia, 26
School nurse, 43
SCOPE, 50
SENSE, 50
Shared parental leave, 67
Short-term Breaks, 124
Siblings, 21
Social worker (Childrens), 4, 35
Special Educational Needs (SEN), 103
Specialised activities, 32
State pension, 76
Statutory maternity pay, 56
Statutory maternity leave, 56
Statutory paternity pay, 62
Still births, 68
Stroke, 26
Systemic lupus erythematosis, 26

Tax Credits, 80
The Blue Badge Scheme, 114
The Royal Institute for Blind People, 49
Thrombosis, 26
Transition Information Network, 51

Transport, 113

Universal Credit, 77

War pensioners mobility supplement, 116
Welfare benefits, 113
Wheelchairs, 120
Work programmes, 136
Working tax credit, 81

****

www.straightforwardco.co.uk

All titles, listed below, in the Straightforward Guides Series can be purchased online, using credit card or other forms of payment by going to www.straightfowardco.co.uk A discount of 25% per title is offered with online purchases.

Law

A Straightforward Guide to:

Consumer Rights
Bankruptcy Insolvency and the Law
Employment Law
Private Tenants Rights
Family law
Small Claims in the County Court
Contract law
Intellectual Property and the law
Divorce and the law
Leaseholders Rights
The Process of Conveyancing
Knowing Your Rights and Using the Courts
Producing Your own Will
Housing Rights
The Bailiff the law and You
Probate and The Law
Company law
What to Expect When You Go to Court

Give me Your Money-Guide to Effective Debt Collection
Rights of Disabled people

General titles

Letting Property for Profit
Buying, Selling and Renting property
Buying a Home in England and France
Buying and Selling a Property Abroad
Bookkeeping and Accounts for Small Business
Creative Writing
Freelance Writing
Writing Your own Life Story
Writing Performance Poetry
Writing Romantic Fiction
Essay Writing
Speech Writing
the Crime Writers Casebook
Being a Detective
A Comprehensive Guide to Arrest and Detention
A Comprehensive Guide to Burglary and Robbery
A Comprehensive Guide to Drink and Disorder
Creating a Successful Commercial Website
The Straightforward Business Plan
The Straightforward C.V.
Successful Public Speaking
Handling Bereavement
Individual and Personal Finance
Understanding Mental Illness